EXCEPTIONAL
WATCHES

'Take your pleasure seriously.'
Charles Eames

CLÉMENT MAZARIAN

EXCEPTIONAL WATCHES

From the Rolex Daytona to the Casio G-Shock, 90 rare & collectible watches explored

PHOTOGRAPHY BY
HENRY LEUTWYLER

MITCHELL BEAZLEY

PREFACE
BY MARC BEAUGÉ

For a long time, I looked for reasons not to like watches, and for several years, I even found some. One day, a particular model would seem extremely pretentious to me. The next day, another seemed too discreet. There were watches that were too complicated, and others that were too simple. Some were too expensive, and others too cheap. When someone talked about dive watches, I replied that I would rather stay on the surface. If they showed me a chronograph, I said I had all the time in the world. And when I was shown a military watch, I was a pacifist.

I always had a reason not to like watches. But with time, and as a result of various encounters, travel and reading, I eventually came to understand that none of them really made sense. I simply did not know how to look at watches.

A watch is neither a tool nor a fashion accessory. It is not a piece of jewellery nor an object of speculation. It is not defined by its appearance, size or date of manufacture – nor even by its resale value, as a growing number would have us believe. Neither is it defined by its various complexities, which are inevitably paltry in comparison to the capabilities of a computer, or even a mobile phone. In reality, what matters here is everything that cannot be seen. Something that does not appear on a specification sheet, and on which it is impossible to put a price... Behind every watch there is always heritage, culture and expertise. There are also icons and mysteries. And, of course, there are the sounds of the second hand and the winding mechanism.

And finally there is the vocabulary. Flyback, phase of the moon, date, dead second, power reserve indicator, tourbillon... Is there anything more romantic?

Behind a watch there are often hidden stories. The stories of those who made it and those who wore it. From the watchmaker to the diver, from the astronaut to the collector, from father to son – even from buyer to thief – a watch does not age. As it is handed on and as it travels, from the Joux valley in Switzerland to the saleroom, from the depths of the ocean to the moon, and from the pages of a catalogue to those of this book, a watch only gains in substance.

Therein lies the complete beauty of watches – as long as we know how to look at them, they will never die.

FOREWORD

Centuries, even millennia, of technical innovation have gone into the making of watches as we know them today. Complex and aesthetically pleasing, they are the work of highly qualified craftspeople who possess exceptional skills. But in the era of the smartwatch, what makes mechanical watches useful? Why do they fascinate us? Perhaps it is because, along with clothes, they are the most intimate objects in our life. Maybe another reason is that some of them have taken part in extraordinary human adventures. And perhaps it is also because some watches would never have seen the light of day were it not for the perseverance and imagination of a great celebrity. Do we truly possess a watch or are we merely passing it on to future generations? Most of the models examined here will outlive us, despite the scars left by the passage of time. Indeed, the watches featured in this book are essentially old, bear a patina and imperfect – but, put simply, they have lived.

In this book, which is midway between an art book and a book on watchmaking, I invite the reader to discover the cult watches of today. From the first wristwatch to quartz watches, chronographs and dive watches, each is historically, mechanically or simply aesthetically interesting. But to be clear – my intention is not to list basic facts or produce a guide for well-informed collectors. Some of the text is technical, some is lighter or more personal, but this is first and foremost an enjoyable read about all the aspects of the sometimes closed world of watchmaking and collecting.

As for the watches I have included, I have been as objective as possible, but it is nevertheless a personal selection. Although the watches shown do not, sadly, belong to me, this book showcases my dream collection. Some readers will unquestionably feel that certain models are missing. They are probably right; there are so many watches out there. However, the various watches that have left their mark on our era are well represented. Each photograph of these timepieces, which belong to collectors or dealers who are friends of mine, is the work of Henry Leutwyler, an acclaimed still-life specialist, who seemed the obvious partner for this book. There are very few images that show a watch displaying the time at 10 minutes past 10, as is the norm. This is deliberate: it is a matter of both observing the instant and the passing of time and of giving a certain rhythm to this book, which aims to be different from a mere catalogue.

So, this is an invitation for you to join me on a journey through time and the various complexities of the watch. Or if you prefer, you have just acquired a very fine doorstop for your library. Simply browse through this book as you please and seek out what tempts you.

TIMELINE

From the first Santos-Dumont made by Cartier in 1904
to Swatch's Moonswatch in 2022, the history of watches is a rich one.
Take a look back over many years of exceptional
watchmaking creativity and skill.

| 1904 | CARTIER | SANTOS-DUMONT |

| 1917 | CARTIER | TANK |

| 1926 | ROLEX | OYSTER |

| 1931 | JAEGER-LECOULTRE | REVERSO
—
ROLEX | OYSTER PERPETUAL |

| 1932 | PATEK PHILIPPE | CALATRAVA |

| 1933 | INGERSOLL | MICKEY MOUSE |

| 1936 | BOVET | MONO-RATTRAPANTE
—
UNIVERSAL GENÈVE | COMPAX
1964: The 'Nina Rindt' models were launched |

| 1944 | UNIVERSAL GENÈVE
TRI-COMPAX |

| 1945 | ROLEX | DATEJUST |

| 1947 | VULCAIN | CRICKET |

| 1948 | OMEGA | SEAMASTER |

| 1952 | OMEGA | CONSTELLATION |

| 1953 | BLANCPAIN | FIFTY FATHOMS
—
BREITLING | CO-PILOT
—
ROLEX | EXPLORER
—
ROLEX | SUBMARINER
Launched in Basel in 1954 |

| 1954 | BREITLING | NAVITIMER
—
ROLEX | GMT MASTER
—
TUDOR
OYSTER PRINCE SUBMARINER
—
TYPE 20
—
UNIVERSAL GENÈVE | POLEROUTER |

| 1956 | JAEGER-LECOULTRE
MEMOVOX AUTOMATIQUE
Jaeger-LeCoultre Memovox
mechanical from 1950
—
ROLEX | DAY-DATE
—
ROLEX | MILGAUSS
Prototypes for CERN researchers
from 1954 |

| 1957 | OMEGA | SPEEDMASTER
—
OMEGA | SEAMASTER 300
—
OMEGA | RAILMASTER
—
HAMILTON | VENTURA |

| 1958 | ETERNA | KONTIKI
—
OMEGA | RANCHERO |

| 1960 | BLANCPAIN | AIR COMMAND
—
BULOVA | ACCUTRON
—
ENICAR | SHERPA GRAPH
—
ENICAR | SHERPA GUIDE
—
WAKMANN
TRIPLE CALENDAR
—
WITTNAUER
SUPER COMPRESSOR
Compressor patents registered
in 1953 |

| 1961 | NIVADA | CHRONOMASTER (CASD)
—
TIMEX | ELECTRIC |

| 1962 | HEUER | AUTAVIA
—
JEANRICHARD/
AQUASTAR AIRSTAR
—
PATEK PHILIPPE
CALENDRIER PERPÉTUEL
AUTOMATIQUE
1925: First wristwatch with
perpetual date
(No. 97 975)
1941: First production mechanical
wristwatch with perpetual date
(ref. 1526) |

| 1963 | HEUER | CARRERA
—
ROLEX | COSMOGRAPH DAYTONA |

| 1964 | WITTNAUER | 242 T |

| 1967 | DOXA | SUB
—
HEUER | BUNDESWEHR
—
OMEGA | DE VILLE
—
ROLEX | SEA-DWELLER
—
YEMA | YACHTINGRAF |

| 1968 | PATEK PHILIPPE | ELLIPSE |

| 1969 | OMEGA | FLIGHTMASTER
—
ZENITH | EL PRIMERO
1969-01-10
—
HEUER | MONACO
Cal. 11 – a rival to El Primero
1969-03-03 |

| 1970 | TUDOR | HOMEPLATE |

| 1971 | OMEGA | SEAMASTER 600 PLOPROF
Prototype from 1968
—
ROLEX | EXPLORER II |

| 1972 | AUDEMARS PIGUET | ROYAL OAK
First design produced 1970
Prototype from 1971
—
HAMILTON | PULSAR
Prototype from 1970 |

| 1975 | LIP | MACH 2000 |

| 1976 | IWC | GAMME SL
Ingenieur model launched 1955
—
PATEK PHILIPPE | DUAL TIME
—
PATEK PHILIPPE | NAUTILUS |

| 1977 | ROLEX | OYSTERQUARTZ
Beta21 movement used by Rolex in
a thousand models from 1970
—
VACHERON CONSTANTIN | 222 |

| 1979 | SEIKO | WORLD TIME 'WOPR'
1969: Seiko created the first quartz
watch – the Astron |

| 1983 | CASIO | G-SHOCK
—
SWATCH
1990: Chrono line launched |

| 1987 | FLIK FLAK |

| 1992 | VACHERON CONSTANTIN
RÉPÉTITION MINUTE
1941: First wristwatch featuring
a minute repeater by Vacheron
Constantin |

| 2000 | BREGUET | LUNE ASTRONOMIQUE
1780: Invention of the perpetual
calendar watch
1783: Breguet hands and numerals
1786: Engraved dial |

| 2022 | SWATCH | MOONSWATCH |

TIME MEASURED THROUGH THE AGES

**How was time measured 100, 1,000 or even 10,000 years ago?
Different needs called for different methods.
From the gnomon to the atomic clock, here is a brief history of time.**

THE OBSERVATION OF TIME

From the dawn of time humans have been aware of the regular occurrence of certain phenomena: day, night, rainy seasons, the flowering of plants and the migration of animals – events that are all repeated at regular intervals and that indicated the changing seasons. By day, the sun's position in the sky and its height allowed the solar year to be easily determined. By night, the moon and its phases indicated the lunar month. This is how the first calendars came into being among the ancient Egyptians and the Maya – even though, strictly speaking, this did not involve the measurement of time.

FROM THE GNOMON TO THE SUNDIAL

In antiquity, among the first to be preoccupied with the division of the day into units of time were the Babylonians, who created the gnomon. This was simply a rod planted in the ground which its users observed the shadow it cast. This rudimentary technique was improved with a rod marked with a scale, with the aim of measuring the time that had passed. The Egyptians perfected the gnomon, and made the first sundials: the shadow was projected on to a semicircle marked with points to indicate the time, but not with great accuracy. Sundials were used for several centuries, and although the ancient Greeks improved them by introducing

unequal hours (one twelfth of the hours of daylight, which therefore varied in length throughout the year), divided by a style (a sort of rod), the accuracy varied between different civilizations and types and sizes of sundial. Sundials were still in use during the Middle Ages, when some simply indicated the times when work began and ended on building sites.

THE CLEPSYDRA AND THE HOURGLASS

Sundials needed sunlight in order to work. Night-time and weather led to the invention of a system for calculating intervals in a more regular fashion and that could even be used indoors: the clepsydra. The earliest version appeared around 1600 BCE. Water flowed from one container into a second and even into a third. Thanks to a mechanism, this device, also invented by the ancient Egyptians and perfected by the ancient Greeks, evolved into a water clock that was used until the 16th century. Another invention that enabled people to measure intervals of time was the hourglass. Just like today, this 'mound of lost moments', as Ernst Jünger called it, was of little use for measuring long periods of time and needed to be upturned frequently. It was most widely used from the 14th to the 18th centuries, and most often contained ground eggshells rather than real sand, which was too irregular to measure the hours consistently.

FIRE CLOCKS AND CALIBRATED CANDLES

An instrument that was certainly less accurate than the latest clepsydra, but which allowed the calculation of longer periods of time than an hourglass, was used in China from the 6th century onwards: the fire clock. Sticks of incense, burning at a fixed rate, were arranged on a horizontal base, which was often hollow and made of lacquer. As the sticks burned, they passed a series of marks that made it possible to calculate the time that had elapsed. The calibrated candle, the invention of which is attributed to the English king Alfred the Great (849–899), appeared some time later. This device was designed to be used at night to count the hours that passed between each prayer. A candle around 1m (39in) tall, bearing marks at regular intervals, indicated the number of hours that had passed as it burned down. Three candles were needed to last until dawn. The use of this device, which was inaccurate because of the varying quality of the wax used and the potential for draughts, spread rapidly all over medieval Europe. The candles were later replaced by oil lamps.

BELLS AND MECHANICAL CLOCKS

During the Middle Ages, monks manually rang church bells to announce the hour for prayer and to mark the passing of time during the day. In order to make this task easier, and to prevent it being forgotten,

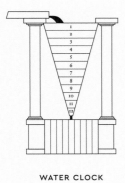

WATER CLOCK

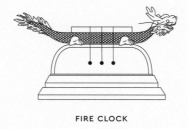

FIRE CLOCK

BELL

the most ingenious monks connected a clepsydra to a hammer which, when the time came, struck a bronze bell. However, such timing devices suffered from the same drawback as clepsydras: the flow of water varied, depending on the temperature and atmospheric pressure, which affected their accuracy. The first mechanical clocks date from the end of the 13th century and are still used to ring church bells today. They initially featured a dial and a single hand, and used the foliot mechanism: the rotation of the hand was driven by a weight attached to a rope that was wound around a horizontal axle. This weight was controlled by a mechanism – the escapement – that blocked its descent for an instant at regular intervals. Relatively accurate, these clocks were often combined with a sundial.

Galileo studied the principles governing the oscillation of a pendulum around the year 1600, but it was the Dutch physicist Huygens who, working with the clockmaker Coster, developed the first clock featuring a pendulum in 1657. This acted as a regulating device, thanks to its constant rate of movement. In 1675, Huygens fitted a spiral spring to this system, which made it possible to reduce the size of the mechanism and build the first tabletop clocks.

POCKET WATCHES – FOLLOWED BY WRISTWATCHES

Fob watches first appeared in Germany during the 15th century, and rapidly won over the wealthy, who wanted to 'wear' the time. They featured spring-driven mechanisms that were perfected during the 18th century. The watchmaker Lépine invented a calibre mounted on a single main plate, allowing the thickness of the watch to be further reduced. Watches whose winding mechanism was positioned at the top of the dial – at 12 o'clock – were known as 'Lépine watches'. This separated them from 'pocket watches' where the winder was positioned at 3 o'clock. At the end of the 18th century, the inventions of Abraham-Louis Breguet (see page 180) revolutionized watchmaking and elevated it to the rank of an art. The use of superior materials, the development of a perpetual automatic movement, repeater watches, the 'pare-chute' shock protection system, the refinement of escapements, the tourbillon and so forth – this watchmaker's creations were prized in all the European courts and culminated in the creation of a masterpiece for the French queen Marie Antoinette in 1783.

Fob watches, which were worn attached to the owner's waistcoat by a chain, became the most widespread type, and remained so until the beginning of the 20th century. The few wristwatches made were reserved for women.

During World War I, wristwatches became popular with soldiers, and subsequently gained popularity away from the battlefield. Initially these were hand-wound, so that they could be reasonably flat. However, later technical innovations allowed flat, automatic watches to be developed.

TECHNOLOGIES

At the beginning of the 20th century the first quartz oscillator appeared. Quartz is a mineral that oscillates at a constant frequency when an electric current is applied to it. The Japanese brand Seiko miniaturized it in the 1970s and marketed it on a large scale through its Astron model. This led to the quartz crisis (see page 209): it took Switzerland's watchmaking industry several decades to recover from that, despite its 'Swiss made' reputation.

ATOMIC TIME

Today the atomic second is the height of accuracy, and international atomic time is the global benchmark. It is calculated by the International Bureau of Weights and Measures in Sèvres, France, and is based on an average calculated from about 500 clocks around the world, each of which features an atom of caesium-133 with a claimed deviation of only 1 second every 300 million years. Of all the instruments for measuring time, these are the most accurate ever made.

MAHATMA GANDHI AND HIS POCKET WATCH

A spiritual guide and the founder of modern India, Mahatma Gandhi believed time to be of great importance. He used a Zenith alarm pocket watch to keep track of it, and the history of this watch is worth repeating.

MAHATMA GANDHI AND THE IMPORTANCE OF TIME

Mahatma Gandhi was born on 2 October 1869 in Porbandar, India. A lawyer, writer, spiritual guide and founder of modern India, Gandhi was renowned for his way of living. He rejected all worldly goods, made his own clothes, prayed regularly and fasted to purify himself or to protest against Britain's subjugation of his country. Although he was not interested in material possessions, Gandhi nevertheless cherished his fob watch, which he did not consider to be decorative in any way. He rose at 4am every day and went to bed at exactly midnight. Time and punctuality were the embodiment of the discipline that he preached to his people. An anecdote told by his grandson Kantilal illustrates this. In 1929, during a train journey, Gandhi asked him the time. The watch displayed the time at 1659, but Kantilal replied that it was 1700. Gandhi was outraged, and said: 'You have absolutely no idea of the value of time! What huge loss might that minute cause our poor people to suffer? You have no respect for truth, even when you know what it is. Would it have been more difficult for you to reply 1659 than to say it was exactly 1700?'

THE INDIAN LEADER'S ZENITH VOX

For a long time, Gandhi's travelling companion was a famous fob watch: a $1 Ingersoll (see page 30). But another watch, given to him by Indira Nehru (his friend, and the woman who went on to be prime minister of India from 1966 to 1977 and 1980 to 1984) was certainly the one he cherished most. It was a Zenith Vox with a sterling silver alarm function and a dial with luminous radium markers. It was no thicker or larger than a normal pocket watch, and was especially useful because it reminded him when to pray and could be read in the dark. But in 1947 it was stolen from him during a journey to Kanpur. Deeply saddened at having lost one of his few possessions (the others were his glasses, his sandals and some tableware), he decided to publish an appeal to the thieves in his newspaper, *Harijan*, in the hope that it might be returned to him. This event was prominently reported by the newspapers, and some British manufacturers sent Gandhi their products. However, he found them too luxurious or ostentatious, and never wore them. Luckily six months later in New Delhi the thief, gripped by remorse, brought the watch back to Gandhi, who received him personally in order to forgive him. Despite his obsession with punctuality,

Mahatma Gandhi was late for prayers at 17:00 on 30 January 1948. The Indian leader was tragically assassinated when he was shot four times by a nationalist. His heart stopped at 17:17; his watch's movement five minutes earlier, at 17:12.

AUCTION IN 2009

In March 2009, despite vehement protests by the Indian government and the country's press, the personal possessions of Mahatma Gandhi, the nation's hero, were put up for auction by Antiquorum in New York. Initially with an estimate of $10,000, the lot (comprising his watch, glasses, sandals and tableware) attracted a bid of $1.8 million in the space of four minutes. The buyer was identified as the Indian billionaire Vijay Vittal Mallya. Gandhi's great-grandson was overjoyed. 'I am relieved that these items have been saved for India, and happy that they are returning to India for future generations of Indians,' he said. Gandhi's iconic alarm pocket watch was thus returned to his homeland, as he probably would have wanted.

ZENITH VOX GANDHI
ALARM POCKET WATCH

Zenith began to market its products in India in 1901. Gandhi was given
one of its pocket watches by his friend Indira Nehru, who was
prime minister of India from 1966 to 1977 and 1980 to 1984.

AT THE HEART OF THE MOVEMENT

FACT SHEET N°1

**The movement is the heart of the watch.
It transforms the energy generated by the winding of a coiled spring –
or a battery in the case of a quartz watch – into regular pulses.
These pulses are transmitted to the display, which indicates the time.**

ENERGY

A watch's energy is supplied by a mechanical spring or a battery. Although they both deliver the same amount of energy, a battery does so at a constant rate; a spring does not provide the same uniformity. Once a mechanical watch has been wound, the spring is at maximum tension and so it releases a lot of force; but subsequently this force diminishes. The skill of the watchmaker lies in obtaining the most stable energy flow possible, from start to finish. The escapement and the winding and setting mechanism ensure that this energy is constant. It should be noted that some mechanical watches feature a power reserve indicator, which displays the amount of energy remaining.

TRANSMISSION AND GEARS

The movement of a watch uses its energy to drive the hands or display figures on the dial. Electric models contain printed circuits that transmit the display. Watches with mechanical movements use a system of gears to perform this function and to connect the barrel, which accumulates the energy, to the winding and setting mechanism.

A gear system generally consists of four wheel trains (five for a watch that runs for a week or longer without needing to be rewound). A train is an assembly consisting of a wheel attached to an axle with a pinion. Such wheels are generally made of brass and have teeth that engage with each wheel train and create gear reduction. The speed of rotation of the various wheel trains corresponds to the different indications of time – that is, hours, minutes and seconds.

THE ESCAPEMENT AND REGULATION VIA A SPIRAL BALANCE

The escapement converts energy into pulses. Today, the lever escapement is by far the most widely used. It is always combined with a regulating mechanism, which divides time into equal segments to ensure the process is constant: this is called a spiral balance. This assembly is of crucial importance – the accuracy of the watch depends upon it.

FREQUENCY

Frequency, which is measured in hertz, refers to the number of oscillations per second. The higher the frequency, the greater the accuracy of the watch. More specifically, the higher the frequency, the more a given period of time is divided up into short pulses. And the more pulses there are, the more accurate the measurement is. Thus a watch beating at 21,600 vibrations per hour (VpH), which is equal to 3 Hz, will be less accurate than one beating at 36,000 VpH (5 Hz).

DISPLAYING THE TIME

The time can be displayed in several ways. Usually this is analogue: the time is shown by the movement of a pointer (the hand) over a scale of hours, minutes and seconds (the dial). It can also be digital, in which case the time is indicated using only figures (for example, the G-Shock – see page 224).

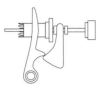

WINDING & SETTING MECHANISM

Allows the barrel to be rewound and the time
to be adjusted (winding stem, pull-out piece,
sliding pinion, winding pinion, lever).

TRAIN WHEELS

Transmits energy from the driving organ to the escapement
and makes the indicator organ (centre wheel, third wheel,
seconds wheel) rotate.

HOUR & MINUTE WHEELS

Display the passing of time
via the movement of the hands
(hours wheel, minutes wheel,
cannon-pinion).

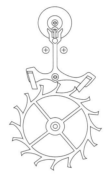

ESCAPEMENT

Counts and maintains the
oscillations (escape wheel,
lever, limiting pins).

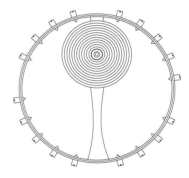

BALANCE WHEEL & BALANCE SPRING

Divides time into equal parts
(spiral balance).

MOVEMENT, DIAL SIDE

MAIN PLATE

BRIDGES

A WELL-CALIBRATED MECHANISM

FACT SHEET N°2

A mechanical movement, also known as a calibre, consists of three parts,
like a sandwich: the lower part is the main plate and the upper part is the bridges.
The moving parts between them are the filling.

MAIN PLATE

This is the base of the movement. Aesthetically, it resembles a coin, with cavities and holes that accommodate the various gears and retaining screws. Gold or rhodium plating are used to protect it from oxidation. The diameter of the main plate dictates the size of the movement. It can be measured in millimetres, but watchmakers use another unit of measurement: the ligne. One ligne is equivalent to 2.256mm.

MOVING COMPONENTS

The gears and other moving elements are usually sited at the heart of the movement, although some of them are sometimes located outside in order to highlight them. The gears are the watch's transmission system; they relay the energy accumulated in the barrel to the escape wheel. Within the bridges and under pressure from the mainspring, the barrel rotates and causes the gears to turn. The first gear wheel, immediately after the barrel, is the centre wheel, situated at the centre of the movement. It makes one revolution every 12 hours and drives the hour hand. The second gear wheel is the intermediate wheel. The third wheel relates to seconds. It may be found either in the centre of the

movement or at the 6 o'clock position. It makes one revolution every 60 seconds and drives the second hand, if the watch has one. These three gear wheels are made of brass. The fourth wheel is the escape (or anchor) wheel; it is not part of the gears, but belongs to the escapement. It releases the energy transmitted via the gears to the anchor in an intermittent fashion. This wheel differs from the three previous ones because it is made of steel, so that it can withstand the shock of contact with the anchor. On the dial side, the small toothed wheel that supports the minute hand adjoins the shaft of the central pinion. It engages with the minutes wheel, which bears the minutes pinion and which, in turn, engages with the hours wheel.

BRIDGES

These metal components are part of the *ébauche* (a complete, unassembled watch movement), and are located above the moving components, which they keep in place. They are made from the same material as the main plate, and are machined and drilled. A bridge is a plate fixed to the main plate, and it is the element on which one of the pivots of the moving parts of the movement turns. The two extremities of the bridge are attached to the main plate by screws.

A mechanical watch features several bridges. They are called bridges because of the function they perform: the barrel bridge (the upper part of which brings together the elements that link the barrel with the winding stem), the bridge that supports the gears (the seconds, centre and third wheels), and the bridge that bears the escape wheel. These elements are sometimes assembled as a single piece. The balance cock, on which the index (regulator) is mounted, controls the speed at which the watch runs, and is sometimes simply referred to as the 'cock'.

Bridges are sometimes adorned with decoration: *côtes de Genève*, chamfering or other engraving. Although today they are purely structural elements of a calibre, the role of which is to ensure the mechanism is rigid, they are the object of much aesthetic embellishment by watchmakers. As regards the dial, a very small number of makers have truly made the bridges a signature design; Richard Mille and Roger Dubuis spring to mind. As regards the movement, the shape and configuration of these are akin to an identity document photograph of the movement. Experts and the most well-informed collectors can immediately recognize a make or a specific movement just by looking at them.

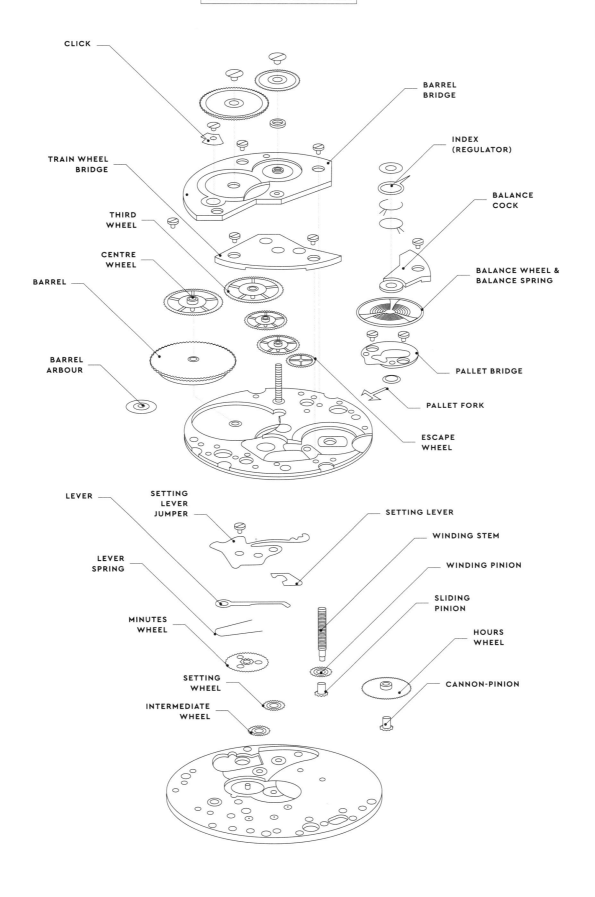

EXPLODED VIEW OF A MOVEMENT

CLICK

BARREL BRIDGE

INDEX (REGULATOR)

TRAIN WHEEL BRIDGE

BALANCE COCK

THIRD WHEEL

CENTRE WHEEL

BALANCE WHEEL & BALANCE SPRING

BARREL

BARREL ARBOUR

PALLET BRIDGE

PALLET FORK

ESCAPE WHEEL

LEVER

SETTING LEVER JUMPER

SETTING LEVER

WINDING STEM

WINDING PINION

LEVER SPRING

SLIDING PINION

HOURS WHEEL

MINUTES WHEEL

SETTING WHEEL

CANNON-PINION

INTERMEDIATE WHEEL

CASE, GLASS AND CROWN

FACT SHEET N°3

A watch is made up of a clearly defined ensemble of components. Once you understand their purpose you will start to understand the well-oiled mechanism that drives your watch.

GLASS

The glass or crystal protects the watch – especially the dial – from water and dirt. The development of different treatment techniques has enabled manufacturers to make high-quality glass that can withstand impact, scratches, pressure and extreme temperatures. There are three main categories:

- **Acrylic crystal (Plexiglas)**: although it scratches and breaks easily, it can be polished and is easy to replace.
- **Mineral crystal**: does not withstand scratching well, but is more resistant to impact than Plexiglas and is not affected by ultraviolet light.
- **Sapphire crystal**: this synthetic glass has the same properties as naturally occurring sapphire. Though highly resistant to scratching, it can become dull or shatter on impact.

CASE

The case is the watch's shell. It must be resistant to impact and sudden movement, as well as waterproof to prevent liquids or dust from getting into it. Every case has at least one opening to allow the mechanism to be adjusted – most often the crown on the side. However, some watches are adjusted from the back or via the bezel. A case possesses two fundamental characteristics: ergonomics and aesthetic appeal. Although most watches on the market are circular, there are several other shapes:

- **Round**: the most common shape is also the easiest for reading the time.
- **Square**: less conventional, the square or rectangular case occupies an important place in the history of watchmaking.
- **Tonneau**: French for 'barrel', this shape, much loved by the fashion-conscious, resembles a spindle with the ends cut off.
- **Cushion**: this shape is an amalgam of round and square.
- **Free**: manufacturers let their imagination run free.
  Patek Philippe produced the Ellipse (see page 38) in 1968, and Hamilton launched the Ventura model with a triangular case (see page 204) in 1957.

LUGS

These are the two protrusions on the case, between which the strap is attached.

BEZEL

The bezel is the ring that surrounds the glass on the top of the case. Most often it helps to ensure that it is waterproof. It also plays a part in the style and function of the watch. Thus, dive watches feature a rotating, calibrated bezel, and chronographs such as the Speedmaster display a tachymeter on the bezel; the Royal Oak's octagonal bezel with eight screws is a signature design feature.

CROWN AND PUSH-BUTTONS

The crown adjusts the functions of a watch and activates the winding mechanism on manual models. It is used to adjust the basic functions of the watch – time, date and phases of the moon. In waterproof models it may be screwed on, in which case it is designed like a bolt. It has a thread inside and screws on to a microtube that protrudes from the case.

The complexities of a chronograph require push-buttons. The first of these is located above the crown and the second below it. This button is fitted with a spring that causes it to return outwards, back to its original position. Sometimes, the buttons are integrated with the crown, as in the case of some one-button chronographs. They must never be activated while diving, because there is a risk that the waterproofing of the watch will be compromised.

THE PARTS OF A WATCH

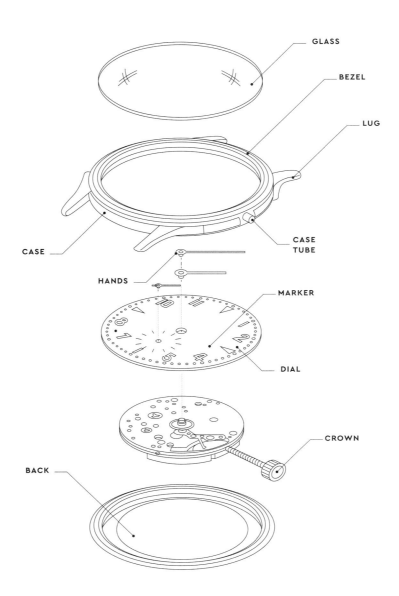

GLASS

BEZEL

LUG

CASE

CASE TUBE

HANDS

MARKER

DIAL

CROWN

BACK

CASE SHAPES

ROUND

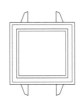

SQUARE

TONNEAU

CUSHION

TRIANGLE OR VENTURA

THE DIAL, HANDS AND CASEBACK

**The back of a watch is the bottom of the case,
which may be engraved and is sometimes transparent.
The dial is the face of the watch and the hands bring it to life.**

DIAL AND MARKERS

The dial is the face of the watch. It allows the owner to read the time in the blink of an eye, and displays information about the model, such as the brand or its functions. The design and construction of a dial differ between models. Dials are usually flat and may feature windows – apertures – that display the date. But they may equally well be convex or concave: the Omega Constellation (see page 60) has a 'pie pan' dial with 12 facets, which is raised in the centre. Sometimes they feature several levels, especially in the case of chronographs, which display subsidiary dials. In that case, the surface is not flat but features some raised areas like a coin. Some dials also feature measuring scales, designed to enhance the functionality of the watch (see page 102). Finally, they may be decorated with surface treatments such as lacquering (see page 102) or engine turning, an artisanal engraving method performed using a hand-operated machine that produces symmetrical and geometric patterns featuring motifs resembling tapestry or grains of barley (*grain d'orge*), lines, *clous de Paris*, or concentric, *flinqué* motifs. Dials have markers, which are generally made of steel, but certain luxury watches feature markers made of precious stones. They are sometimes covered with a luminous material: originally this was radium, subsequently tritium, now replaced by luminova.

They may be different shapes, such as rectangles, triangles or simply points. They may also take the form of Arabic or Roman numerals.

HANDS

The hands bring the watch to life. Their chief function is to convey the time, via their movement in conjunction with the markers on the dial. The first watches had only one hand – an hour hand. The introduction of the minute hand, in around 1691, is attributed to the English watchmaker Daniel Quare. Today, watches generally have three hands, indicating the hours, minutes and seconds, but may also feature others, depending on the model's functions (GMT, for example). They constitute powerful visual signals, and their design may be typical of a manufacturer (as in the case of the hands of Omega's Broad Arrow, and those of Breguet and Rolex Mercedes). Although the commonest shape for a hand is that of a baton, there are many other kinds, such as leaves or the dauphine style. The length and shape of the hands also play a part in their function. It is well known that the hour hand is shorter than the minute hand. But certain designs enhance the functionality of a watch in specific ways. For example, engineers at Doxa made the minute hand on the Sub model broader, so as to offer even more visibility to divers when making calculations during their underwater sessions.

THE CASEBACK

It should be remembered that the case protects the watch's movement from dust, damp and impact. The caseback is on the opposite side to the dial, and acts like a lid to enclose the case and protect the inside of the watch. Some are transparent, in order to display the movement, but most are made of solid metal, and some are decorated or engraved. These engravings may be mass-produced (from 1969, Speedmaster watches featured an engraving commemorating the moon landing) or owners may have them created by craftsmen. The inside of the caseback contains information on the make, and the watch's serial or reference number. It may also display marks made by the watchmaker. Until the 1930s, watchmakers used coded initials to engrave details of the repair work carried out on movements. Some craftsmen continue this practice. On the inside of the caseback of an old watch it is not unusual to find a discreet engraving recording work carried out with the date it took place.

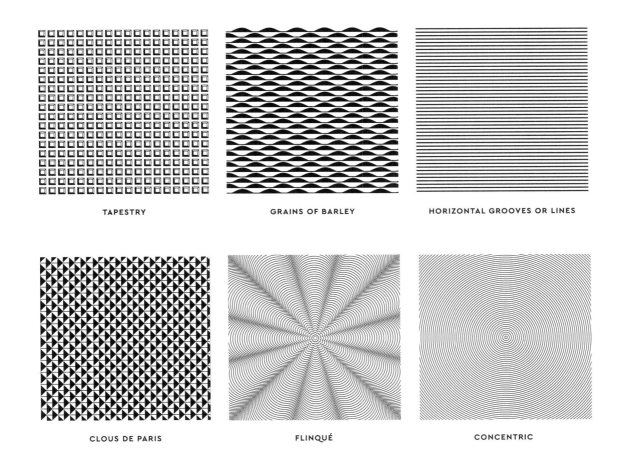

TAPESTRY

GRAINS OF BARLEY

HORIZONTAL GROOVES OR LINES

CLOUS DE PARIS

FLINQUÉ

CONCENTRIC

HANDS

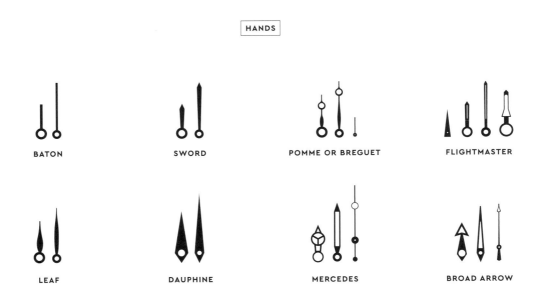

BATON

SWORD

POMME OR BREGUET

FLIGHTMASTER

LEAF

DAUPHINE

MERCEDES

BROAD ARROW

MECHANICAL
WATCHES

CHAPTER 1

KINETIC ENERGY

FACT SHEET N°5

**In order to function, a mechanical watch requires kinetic energy.
This energy is supplied to the mechanism by a spring, which is coiled when the watch is wound.
It sits within a small cylindrical case called a barrel.**

HOW A MECHANICAL WATCH WORKS

A mechanical watch functions on a mechanical movement which, among other things, consists of a mainspring (the energy reserve), an escapement (often with a lever) and a regulator (the spiral balance). This therefore differs from a watch with an electronic movement, which requires a battery to function.

In order to understand how mechanical energy works, a parallel can be drawn with a child's clockwork toy car, which is wound with a key and runs until its energy has been used up. A mechanical watch works in the same way, except that its reserve of energy lasts longer, thanks to the combination of the escapement and the winding and setting mechanism (unlike a toy car, whose energy runs out quickly).

BARREL

The energy of a mechanical watch is stored in a combination of components, consisting of a toothed wheel and a cylindrical container closed with a barrel cap. The mainspring, a long, flexible steel ribbon, is wound around the barrel's arbour by the winding mechanism. It is located in a container known as the drum. Once rewound, the mainspring is coiled and uncoiled more

than 300 times a year. This happens with considerable force to produce the energy required for the watch to work. When a watch is rewound, the mainspring is wound around the barrel arbour, which accumulates energy; this will be transmitted to the gearing as long as it lasts.

MAINSPRING

The mainspring is the watch's reserve of mechanical energy. It took several centuries for a reliable one to be developed. Today, the mainspring, which has a reversed S-shape, consists of a ribbon of hardened and blued steel or of a specialized alloy, often pre-lubricated on assembly. It is rolled up inside the barrel and has a high degree of shape memory. The length of the mainspring depends on the thickness of the ribbon and the diameter of the barrel. The uncoiling of the ribbon produces the energy required for the watch to function. After many years, when the mainspring is 'tired' – has lost elasticity – the only way to ensure the watch continues to work properly is to replace it.

THE ACCURACY OF A MECHANICAL WATCH

The escapement, usually a lever escapement, is a device located between the gearing and the balance. Its function is to interrupt the movement of the gears at regular intervals and periodically supply energy to the balance. The winding and setting mechanism – the balance – consists of a wheel with two or three arms, which is statically balanced and coupled with a spiral (steel spring). It rotates back and forth and divides time into equal units. The combination of the escapement and the mechanism ensures that a mechanical watch is accurate.

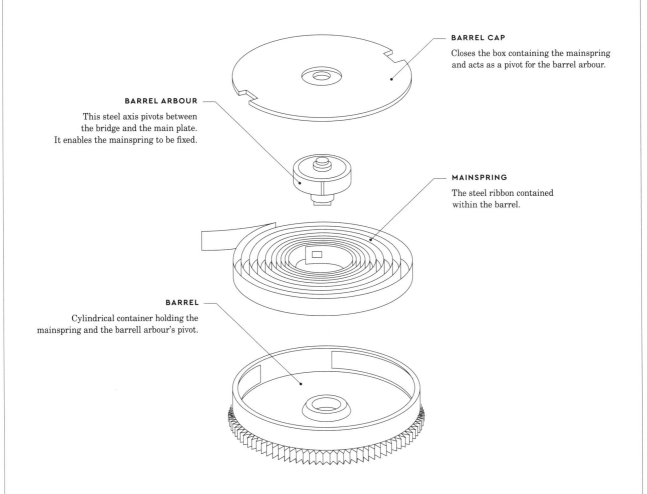

BARREL CAP

Closes the box containing the mainspring
and acts as a pivot for the barrel arbour.

BARREL ARBOUR

This steel axis pivots between
the bridge and the main plate.
It enables the mainspring to be fixed.

MAINSPRING

The steel ribbon contained
within the barrel.

BARREL

Cylindrical container holding the
mainspring and the barrell arbour's pivot.

CAP
(SEEN FROM ABOVE)

ARBOUR
(SEEN FROM ABOVE)

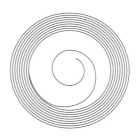

MAINSPRING CONTAINED WITHIN THE BARREL
(SEEN FROM ABOVE)

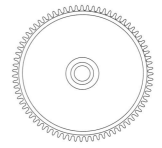

BARREL
(SEEN FROM ABOVE)

MECHANICAL WATCHES

HAND-WOUND

When the movement is wound by hand using the crown, the watch is described as hand-wound.

WINDING BY HAND

As its name indicates, a hand-wound watch draws its energy from being wound by hand – a simple act and a daily ritual. This type of movement requires rewinding every day, ideally at the same time. This operation simply entails turning the crown clockwise until a slight resistance is felt, indicating that rewinding is complete. It is important not to force this – doing so risks damaging the movement.

INVENTION OF THE CROWN BY JOHN ARNOLD

With a hand-wound system, energy is transmitted to the movement from an outside source. Old pocket watches required a key to rewind the movement. In 1820, British watchmaker John Arnold invented an external component that allowed the owner to rewind the barrel: the crown (see page 20), also known as the winding mechanism. Today it is common, and is usually located on the right of the case, at the 3 o'clock position. Its functions are rewinding the mechanism and adjusting the date and, of course, the time. In order to wind the mainspring, it must be turned backwards and forwards. It should be noted that even with an automatic watch, turning the crown coils the mainspring, but it will do so endlessly – unlike on a mechanical watch, where there is resistance after a time.

CONTINUED PRODUCTION

Despite the invention of automatic wristwatches in the 1920s, many manufacturers have continued to produce hand-wound mechanical watches, so as not to make their watches thicker. The first ultra-thin automatic movement was developed by Piaget. In 1957, it won fame with its 9P ultra-fine mechanical calibre, hand-wound watch. Three years later, Piaget launched the 12P automatic calibre, with a thickness of just 2.3mm. This feat was achieved thanks to the use of a micro-rotor system, first developed by Universal Genève and Büren in the mid-1950s. However, few watches with micro-rotors were made available on the market. Hand-winding was often preferred, because it ensured that slender, elegant watches could be manufactured. Even today, the title of 'the world's flattest watch' is fought over at every watchmaking trade fair. Hand-winding allows records to be broken, thanks especially to technologies that combine the calibre with the watch's external parts. In July 2022, the latest hand-wound watch was a Richard Mille RM UP-01 Ferrari that was just 1.75mm thick.

DECORATING THE MOVEMENT

The attraction of good design, which attaches importance to the thickness of a timepiece, can also be found in the heart of a watch: in the decoration of the movement. At first, watchmakers added such finishing touches to erase the marks left by machines or tools during manufacturing. This is still the case, but these have been elevated to an artform. Whether decorated with motifs or polished, some mechanisms are true works of art, even though most of the time, unless the caseback is transparent, their decoration remains hidden.

The different kinds of finishing touches include: chamfering, which involves smoothing the edges between surfaces; circular graining, which produces small circles on the metal's surface by abrasion; and the prestigious *côtes de Genève* – the creation of a series of slightly concave bands, often linear and parallel. With regards to the latter, some experts claim that the bands can trap dust particles, preventing them getting into the movement.

MICKEY MOUSE

INGERSOLL – 1933

**In the 1930s, Ingersoll was the first company to be granted
a licence by Walt Disney to use the image of Mickey Mouse
on its watches. The company sold more than 5 million of them.**

SEE OPPOSITE	1935 MODEL
MANUFACTURER	INGERSOLL
MODEL	MICKEY MOUSE
REFERENCE	N/A
DIAL	WHITE
WINDING MECHANISM	MECHANICAL
CALIBRE	INGERSOLL
DIAMETER	31MM
MATERIAL	CHROME
STRAP	LEATHER, EMBOSSED WITH IMAGE OF MICKEY MOUSE
TYPE	SIMPLE

INGERSOLL'S BEGINNINGS: THE DOLLAR WATCH

The Ingersoll Watch Company was originally a mail order business (R H Ingersoll & Bro), founded in New York in 1882 by Robert Hawley Ingersoll and his brother Charles Henry. Initially, the company manufactured and sold low-cost items such as rubber stamps. Four years later it launched its first watch, the Yankee. It was priced at $1, equivalent to the average daily wage at the time.

By 1910, the Waterbury Clock Company, which made watches for Ingersoll, was producing almost 3.5 million watches a year. The company capitalized on this via numerous advertisements, and came up with the slogan: 'The watch that made the dollar famous!' Theodore Roosevelt himself claimed that, during one of his journeys in Africa, he was referred to as 'the man from the country where Ingersoll is made' – proof of the brand's fame at the time.

FIRST OFFICIAL LICENCE FOR MICKEY MOUSE

So great was its success that Ingersoll took over some of its own suppliers in order to grow the company and broaden its expertise. On the British market, it launched the Crown pocket watch, priced at 5 shillings, then equivalent to $1. In 1919 it launched the Radiolite, a watch featuring a luminous dial with broad radium markers. During the 1930s, in a new stroke of genius, the company secured the rights from Walt Disney to use the image of Mickey Mouse.

It was a smart move as the character was recognized by 98 per cent of children – more than Father Christmas. During the 15 years that the watch was produced, and before relinquishing its licence, Ingersoll sold more than 5 million Mickey Mouse watches.

MICKEY MOUSE, A WATCHMAKING INSPIRATION

Several companies subsequently used the cartoon character's image, borrowing Ingersoll's concept and using Mickey's arms for the hour and minute hands, including Swatch (see page 212). The watchmaking genius Gérald Genta (see page 190), creator of the Royal Oak and the Nautilus (see pages 192 and 194), created two versions, with a retrograde minute hand and jumping hour, which are highly sought after by collectors, and which have since been reissued by Bulgari who now hold the Genta licence.

SANTOS-DUMONT

CARTIER – 1904

**The Cartier Santos-Dumont was the result of a
friendship between a watchmaker and an aviator.
It is considered to be the first
true man's wristwatch.**

SEE OPPOSITE	1990 MODEL
MANUFACTURER	CARTIER
MODEL	SANTOS-DUMONT
REFERENCE	1575 B
DIAL	ENGRAVED (FLINQUÉ), ROMAN NUMERALS
WINDING MECHANISM	MECHANICAL
CALIBRE	F. PIGUET 21
DIAMETER	27 X 36MM
MATERIAL	PLATINUM
STRAP	LEATHER
TYPE	FOLDING BUCKLE

SANTOS-DUMONT

1904	THE SANTOS LAUNCHED
1911	MASS PRODUCTION BEGINS
1973	NEW COLLECTION
1978	NEW VERSION, WITH VISIBLE SCREWS
1987	SANTOS GALBÉE LAUNCHED
1998	CPCP COLLECTION
2004	SANTOS 100 LAUNCHED
2018	CARTIER SANTOS 2018 LAUNCHED

THE STORY OF A FRIENDSHIP

In 1904, the pilot Alberto Santos-Dumont, who made the first public flight in an aeroplane, asked his friend Louis Cartier to complete a special commission for him. At the time, the request was an unusual one. The custom then was for men to carry pocket watches – wristwatches were reserved for women. But at a party in Paris, the aviator complained that pocket watches were unreliable and he could not use one when he was flying.

THE FIRST WRISTWATCH EVER MADE

Cartier took this observation very seriously and, assisted by the master watchmaker Edmond Jaeger, found a solution: a prototype wristwatch that could be read by the pilot while his hands grasped the controls. Louis Cartier then designed a prototype with a strap, which was flat and had a square dial. The first true men's wristwatch – indeed, probably the first pilot's watch – had been invented. A small number were sold, thanks to the two men's renown in Paris during the Belle Époque, then production began in earnest in 1911. A few thousand were sold between then and 1970. Subsequently, many different variations of the model were produced.

SUCCESSFUL VARIANTS

In 1973, 12 models went on the market as part of the new Louis Cartier collection; one of them was the Santos model.

In 1978, a new version was launched at Le Bourget. Cartier redesigned the model, with an integrated strap and visible screws, while at the same time retaining its art deco look. Already popular among discerning customers, this watch was a hit with businessmen during the 1980s. The perfect example? Michael Douglas wore a gold version of this model in the movie *Wall Street*, directed by Oliver Stone. It was also made in a gold and steel version, which was a novelty at the time.

The model evolved further. In 1987, Cartier launched the Galbée. Some models were part of the 1998 CPCP collection; they were available as either a gold or a platinum version. The Santos 100 was introduced in 2004, to celebrate the 100th anniversary of the first watch. In 2018, Cartier created a new version of its iconic model.

Whatever the version, more than a century after its creation this watch – the result of a vision by two enthusiasts – is still hugely successful.

TANK

CARTIER – 1917

**Over the years, and thanks to its geometric watches, Cartier
established itself as a watchmaker that created unique shapes.
The most iconic is unquestionably the Tank.**

SEE OPPOSITE	1978 MODEL
MANUFACTURER	CARTIER
MODEL	TANK LC
REFERENCE	78086
DIAL	WHITE, ROMAN NUMERALS
WINDING MECHANISM	MECHANICAL
CALIBRE	78
DIAMETER	23 X 30MM
MATERIAL	GOLD
STRAP	LEATHER
TYPE	FOLDING BUCKLE

TANK

1917	TANK NORMALE 'WITH ROUNDED EDGES'
1919	OFFICIALLY GOES ON SALE
1921	TANK CINTRÉE
1922	TANK CHINOISE
1924	THE TANK NORMALE BECOMES THE TANK LC (LOUIS CARTIER)
1928	TANK À GUICHETS
1932	TANK BASCULANTE
1973	NEW CARTIER COLLECTION
1977	TANK MUST
1989	TANK AMÉRICAINE
1996	TANK FRANÇAISE

INSPIRED BY A REAL TANK

After creating the Santos-Dumont, Louis Cartier (assisted by Edmond Jaeger) established his reputation as a watchmaker who created unique shapes, thanks to the unusual geometric designs of his watches; these included the Tonneau and the Tortue, so named because of their appearance (a 'barrel' and a 'turtle' respectively). The iconic Tank appeared in 1917, a year before the armistice. Initially known as 'normal' or 'rounded-edges', this watch, which is the manifestation of elegance, was paradoxically inspired by a steel monster: the Allies' Renault FT-17 battle tank seen from above. The Tank was rectangular, its shape seemingly compressed between its straight sides that extended to the point where the strap was fastened. Its crown had a decorative sapphire head and the dial featured a railway track design and Roman numerals. The first Tank was given to the great American soldier General Pershing, and Cartier began to market it in 1919. The Cintrée appeared in 1921, and a smaller version, the Chinoise, in 1922.

DIFFERENT VERSIONS WORN BY THE STARS

In 1924, the watch was officially named the Tank LC (standing for Louis Cartier) and it quickly became popular with people in the arts world. In 1926, in the movie *The Son of the Sheik*, the actor Rudolph Valentino even managed to persuade the director to let him keep his watch on, despite it being an anachronism. This iconic model endured throughout the century and numerous versions appeared on celebrities' wrists.

Duke Ellington, the American jazz composer, wore a Tank à guichets in 1928. In 1932, a model with a pivoting case – the Basculante – appeared on the wrist of the actor Gary Cooper. Steve McQueen sported a Cintrée version in *The Thomas Crown Affair* in 1968. The list of celebrities who contributed to building the legend include, among others, Clark Gable, Stewart Granger, Yves Montand, Alain Delon, Muhammad Ali, Yves Saint Laurent and Andy Warhol, who did not rewind his.

THE PRIVILEGED CHOICE OF FREE WOMEN AND MEN

The former American first lady Jackie Kennedy, an enduring fashion icon, wore an elegant gold version all her life. The watch appears in many famous photographs and was recently bought at auction by Kim Kardashian for £298,500 ($379,500). Diana, Princess of Wales owned two versions, one of which recently reappeared on the wrist of the Duchess of Sussex. The Tank has also been the watch of choice for Catherine Deneuve and Michelle Obama. Truman Capote, flamboyant exponent of New Journalism, owned eight of them, and offered one to a colleague as a replacement for his own, because he did not like the design of it. As Jean-Charles de Castelbajac put it: 'If all tanks were made by Cartier, we would have the time to live in peace.'

CALATRAVA

PATEK PHILIPPE – 1932

**The Calatrava is the quintessential circular wristwatch.
Its appearance coincided with the brand's revival and the
Stern family's acquisition of a stake in the company.**

SEE OPPOSITE	1940 MODEL
MANUFACTURER	PATEK PHILIPPE
MODEL	CALATRAVA
REFERENCE	96
DIAL	SILVER, ARABIC NUMERALS
WINDING MECHANISM	MECHANICAL
CALIBRE	12-120
DIAMETER	31MM
MATERIAL	STEEL
STRAP	GAY FRÈRES
TYPE	BAMBOO

CALATRAVA

1932	REFERENCE 96: CAL. 12-120
1934	REFERENCE 96 D (DECORATED) CLOUS DE PARIS: CAL. 12-120
1953	REFERENCE 2526: CAL. 12-600 AUTOMATIC, 35MM
1972	REFERENCE 3520 D (DECORATED) CLOUS DE PARIS AND ROMAN NUMERALS: CAL. 177 ULTRA-THIN
1985	REFERENCE 3919: CAL. 215, 10 LIGNES

1932, THE STERN BROTHERS ACQUIRE A STAKE IN THE COMPANY

The story of Patek Philippe begins in Geneva in 1839, when Antoine Norbert de Patek, a businessman, and François Czapek, a watchmaker, joined forces to found Patek, Czapek & Cie. Five years later, following some disagreements, the latter made way for the French engineer Jean-Adrien Philippe, who had just won a medal for his keyless winding and adjustment system. The company then became Patek, Philippe & Cie.

Despite having a fine reputation, acquired thanks to numerous watchmaking patents and prestigious clients (from 1851 the company supplied watches to Queen Victoria), Patek Philippe found itself in serious difficulties following the Wall Street Crash in 1929. The company survived and grew thanks to an injection of capital by the brothers Jean and Charles Henri Stern, whose family already owned a factory that made watch dials.

LAUNCH OF THE REFERENCE 96

Although the maker was known for its complications, the brothers decided to broaden their client base by introducing a range of circular, elegant and pared-down wristwatches, in keeping with the company's criteria for excellence. At a time when wristwatches were still a novelty, their use became widespread beyond the battlefields of World War I. Thus the Calatrava range was born in 1932, bearing the reference 96.

The use of the Calatrava name for this collection sheds light on its importance in the eyes of the Stern brothers – the Calatrava cross had been their company's emblem since 1887. It was inspired by the coat of arms of an order of Spanish knights founded in the 12th century, which was known for its values of bravery and independence. The fleurs-de-lis adorning the tips of the cross recall the emblem of the French monarchy.

INSPIRED BY BAUHAUS

The reference 96 was inspired by the Bauhaus movement, the school of architecture and arts founded by Walter Gropius in Germany in 1919. According to this minimalist movement, form follows function. So, while at the height of the art deco period other watchmakers focused on originality, Patek Philippe opted for 'less is more'. There were several types of dial, but the primary function of the watch was reduced to the essential: displaying the time.

The reference 96 was made for more than 40 years, and included a version which had a bezel decorated with *clous de Paris*. The company, which had long resisted the idea of fitting an automatic movement for fear of making the watch thicker, equipped the first versions with a prestigious extra-flat 12 lignes movement.

The slogan that appeared in 1996 – 'You never actually own a Patek Philippe. You merely look after it for the next generation.' – applies *a posteriori* to the Calatrava model.

GOLDEN ELLIPSE

PATEK PHILIPPE – 1968

Constantly seeking innovation, in 1968 Patek Philippe
launched a new range of watches with a divine shape.
Inspired by the golden mean, they departed from conventional standards.

SEE OPPOSITE	1968 MODEL
MANUFACTURER	PATEK PHILIPPE
MODEL	GOLDEN ELLIPSE
REFERENCE	3548
DIAL	GOLD, SIGMA, ROMAN NUMERALS
WINDING MECHANISM	MECHANICAL
CALIBRE	23-300
DIAMETER	27 X 32MM
MATERIAL	GOLD
STRAP	LEATHER
TYPE	SIMPLE

PATEK PHILIPPE
CAL. 23-300

The 23-300 is a calibre of 23mm
(10 lignes), 3mm thick. Thanks
to its compact size, it was often
used from 1956 to 1975.

DIVINE PROPORTIONS

Having set the standard for circular watches
with the Calatrava in 1932, the masterminds
at Patek Philippe turned watch design on
its head with a new collection: the Golden
Ellipse. Unveiled at the 1968 Basel watch fair,
this bold range stood out due to its harmony.
As the name indicates, the shape of the case
is a cross between a circle and a rectangle.
Its design is inspired by the ancient principle
of the golden mean. This divine proportion,
discovered by Greek mathematicians, is
based on the ratio 1:1.6181, and is at the
root of some of the greatest works of art and
architecture in history, represented by the
Fibonacci sequence.

MANY VERSIONS
AND ACCESSORIES

From the 1970s, the Ellipse was a great
success and established itself as an
international symbol of chic. The collection
comprised more than 60 versions: with
various sizes (Brad Pitt owns an old Jumbo
model), different precious metals, leather
and metal straps (braided reeds, chains,
metal mesh), and dials in different colours
(including an iconic cobalt blue) adorned
with markers or Roman numerals. The
elliptical design was also applied to other
case shapes, such as a rectangle and an
octagon, not forgetting the astonishing
Nautilus-Ellipse fusion. The first reference
3548 was fitted with a magnificent
23-300 hand-wound calibre, so as not to
make the watch thicker, but in 1977 the
references 3738 and 3739 were the first to
be fitted with the 240 extra-flat automatic
calibre, which is still used today.

Another interesting fact about the Ellipse is
that it was the first family of watches to be
accompanied by a full range of accessories,
such as cigarette lighters, rings, cufflinks,
clocks and even money clips. At the time,
and today, it embodies the excellence of
Patek Philippe.

AN IMPORTANT COLLECTION
FOR THE STERN FAMILY

This watch, inspired by the golden mean,
occupies a special place in the affections of
the Stern family, which runs the company.
Henri, the CEO at the time, believed that the
firm needed a watch with a unisex design
that was immediately identifiable as a
Patek Philippe. The manufacturer aimed
to create an elegant watch and it turned
out to be revolutionary.

The words of his descendant, Thierry,
marking the 50th anniversary of the
collection, demonstrate the importance of
the Ellipse: 'Every year we discuss ending
production, but we never put that into
practice. We are preserving the spirit of
our grandfather.' It remains part of the
company's range and is its second-oldest
family of watches after the Calatrava.

REVERSO

JAEGER-LECOULTRE – 1931

**It was on a polo field in India that the idea for a watch
with a case that could revolve on its own axis was born:
the Reverso (Latin for 'I turn around').**

MANUFACTURER	JAEGER-LECOULTRE

1. SEE OPPOSITE

MODEL	REVERSO, YEAR 2000
REFERENCE	250286
DIAL	BLACK
WINDING MECHANISM	MECHANICAL
CALIBRE	846/1
DIAMETER	23 × 33MM
MATERIAL	GOLD
STRAP	LEATHER
TYPE	SIMPLE

2. SEE OVERLEAF

MODEL	REVERSO, YEAR 2000
REFERENCE	270862
DIAL	SILVER, TWO-TONE
WINDING MECHANISM	MECHANICAL
CALIBRE	822
DIAMETER	26 × 42MM
MATERIAL	STEEL
STRAP	LEATHER
TYPE	SIMPLE

SPORTING ORIGINS

In 1930, César de Trey, a distributor of Swiss watches, was travelling through the Indian subcontinent, looking to conquer new markets, and saw his first game of polo. This team sport was practised by British army officers and the spectators were drawn from Indian high society. When he examined the players' watches he noticed the glass and dials were damaged and suggested a solution: a way to turn the watch over without the glass coming into contact with the wearer's skin. On his return to Switzerland he entrusted the design of the movement to Jacques-David LeCoultre, who supplied Edmond Jaeger, and that of the case to the engineer René-Alfred Chauvot. In 1931, the latter registered a patent for a 'watch capable of sliding within its support and turning over completely'. The Wenger company was commissioned to manufacture the cases. De Trey and LeCoultre bought the patent and, in order to make their investment profitable, made arrangements for it to be used immediately under licence, including by other manufacturers. The first dials bearing the Jaeger-LeCoultre name appeared in 1937, the year the company was founded.

A WATCH THAT CAN BE PERSONALIZED

The model travelled beyond India and quickly became a success both commercially and in high society, thanks to the ways in which it could be personalized. The dial was initially available in black and silver versions, but red, brown and blue examples were manufactured by the prestigious maker Stern (the future owner of Patek Philippe).

The opportunity to personalize the caseback charmed the middle classes. Owners were bursting with imagination, engraving, enamelling or inscribing mottos on the casebacks of their watches.

CROSSING THE DESERT

The watch business was affected by the end of World War II, when military models flooded the market. The Reverso ended up being discontinued and Wenger disposed of some of its industrial tools. When the quartz crisis hit (see page 209), Jaeger-LeCoultre began to develop new products. In 1972, Giorgio Corvo, a businessman and distributor for the brand in Italy, decided to buy the remaining stock (about 200 items). Despite the manufacturer's scepticism (it requested confirmation of the deal three times) he insisted on relaunching the watch, and identified another manufacturer for its case. In 1975, production tentatively resumed, and the watch became very popular with the Italian jet set. Fiumi, the Milan retailer, set up a visitors' book. Enzo Ferrari, Gianni Versace and Giovanni Agnelli, who was known to like wearing his watch over his shirt cuff, were customers. Boosted by this success, production was reorganized. From 1984, a new catalogue featuring almost 25 examples was devoted to the Reverso. This momentum continued during the 1990s. From the time of the company's acquisition by the Richemont group in 2003 more complications and functions were introduced. However, the timeless Reverso continues to delight watch enthusiasts.

RANCHERO

OMEGA – 1958

Despite a promising launch, the Ranchero was removed from the Omega catalogue after just two years. However, it is especially sought after by collectors today.

SEE OPPOSITE	1958 MODEL
MANUFACTURER	OMEGA
MODEL	RANCHERO
REFERENCE	2990-1
DIAL	WHITE
WINDING MECHANISM	MECHANICAL
CALIBRE	30MM (CAL. 267)
DIAMETER	36MM
MATERIAL	STEEL
STRAP	LEATHER
TYPE	SIMPLE

OMEGA
BROAD ARROW HANDS

A true Omega signature, the broad arrow design, featuring an arrowhead at the end of the hour hand, appeared in 1957, before being used the following year on the Ranchero model.

THE FOURTH MUSKETEER

In 1957, Omega launched a trio of watches: the Speedmaster (ref. 2915), Railmaster (ref. 2914) and Seamaster 300 (ref. 2913). Although the first of these watches was specifically geared for use in motor racing, the second to being antimagnetic and the third to diving, all three were built to the same design. Each featured broad arrow hands – shaped like arrows – the company's signature style.

In 1958, Omega launched its fourth musketeer. Revisiting the design parameters of its elder siblings, the Ranchero was conceived as an entry-level model. At the time it cost 147 Swiss francs (the equivalent of £12 at the time); it was multi-purpose and non-professional and it featured the calibre 267, part of the family of 30mm movements. These were then, and still are, hailed by watchmakers for their accuracy and durability and they are designated according to their diameters. Watches fitted with movements of the 30mm family feature broad cases. That of the Omega Ranchero (36mm) is relatively large for the time.

A COMMERCIAL FAILURE

Despite its broad, watertight case, its rugged manual movement and its chic sports design, the Ranchero was available for only two years. According to the Omega museum, this commercial failure is due to the name that was chosen for the model. The word Ranchero means 'agricultural labourer' in Spanish, which led to a certain resistance in Spanish-speaking countries.

Apart from a brief revival of the name for the Belgian market in the mid-1970s, the model never reappeared in the catalogue.

A HOLY GRAIL FOR COLLECTORS

Since this range was one of Omega's smallest production runs, the Ranchero is naturally very hard to get hold of. Several versions – black or white – exist, but the market is plagued by many dubiously refurbished watches, with repainted dials, poor configurations and so on.

Although the Omega Ranchero was a commercial failure when it was launched, today its design and rarity have earned it the reputation of being a holy grail. More accessible than the Speedmaster, Railmaster and Seamaster 300 from 1957, this watch – a distillation of Omega's know-how at the time – is especially appreciated by enthusiasts.

MECHANICAL WATCHES

AUTOMATIC

The term 'automatic' denotes a watch that requires no action on the user's part to be rewound.

JOHN HARWOOD'S INNOVATION

Watchmaker John Harwood was born in England in 1893. During his studies of watch mechanisms, he became interested in automatic movements. In 1922, after moving to the Isle of Man, he succeeded in developing a mechanism for an automatic wristwatch. However, he had difficulty selling it to the Swiss. Four years later, Harwood registered a patent. He did away with the crown and the winding mechanism; instead an oscillating weight (rotor) rewinds the mechanism, and a notched wheel, driven by a cog, allows the time to be adjusted. This cog was located in the bezel in round models and in the back in square- or cushion-shaped models (see page 20). Despite their innovative nature, their unreliability and – above all – the 1929 economic crisis prevented these models achieving much success.

BUMPER MOVEMENTS

The automatic rewinding system invented by John Harwood was copied by several makers a few years later. Although watch manufacturers have retained the crown system, the mechanism, known as a Bumper movement (see page 58), appealed to large manufacturers such as Universal Genève and Omega. In a Bumper (or hammer) calibre, the oscillating weight does not make a full revolution on its axis: it bumps against springs, thus moving back and forth. Today's free rotors are descended directly from this invention, which was patented in 1924 and mass-produced from 1926.

ROTOR SYSTEM

From the outset, the idea was to use the movement of the wearer's wrist to create energy. The rotor, or oscillating weight, is thus what distinguishes hand-wound watches from automatic ones. This component, invented in the 18th century by Hubert Sarton, is generally made of brass, but on luxury models it may be made of gold or platinum, which are heavier than brass and improve accuracy. The rotor, which varies in size, is a semicircle that rotates around an arbour. It is connected directly to the barrel by a gear wheel. Thus, when the rewinding mechanism of a watch is dependent on wrist movements to cause a rotor to revolve and in turn coil the mainspring, the watch is described as automatic.

MICRO-ROTOR

In the mid-1950s the micro-rotor movement appeared at two companies simultaneously: Universal Genève and Büren. The former called its version Microtor, the latter named it the Planetary Rotor. Unlike standard rotors, they do not rotate outside the movement, but within it. The invention of the micro-rotor helped to make automatic watches thinner. Indeed, Piaget developed an extra-thin – 2.3mm – automatic watch, using a micro-rotor named calibre 12P. However, according to watchmakers, even though modern techniques have made it possible to improve them, these micro-rotors are not as efficient as a normal central rotor. This means that, especially with an old watch, the wearer needs to move more in order for the rotor to wind the watch, which may create problems in getting the watch to start.

OYSTER PERPETUAL

ROLEX – 1931

**If the Rolex brand strikes a chord with watch enthusiasts – and others –
it is partly thanks to the invention of the Oyster,
the first waterproof wristwatch.**

SEE OPPOSITE	1967 MODEL
MANUFACTURER	ROLEX
MODEL	OYSTER PERPETUAL
REFERENCE	1500
DIAL	BLACK, LACQUERED (GILT)
WINDING MECHANISM	AUTOMATIC
CALIBRE	1570
DIAMETER	34MM
MATERIAL	STEEL
STRAP	STEEL
TYPE	OYSTER

OYSTER AND OYSTER PERPETUAL

- **1926** — INVENTION OF THE OYSTER CASE
- **1931** — INVENTION OF THE PERPETUAL ROTOR

ROLEX
PERPETUAL ROTOR

In 1931, Rolex perfected an automatic
winding system that allowed the
watch to be rewound simply
by moving the wrist.

ORIGINS

In 1903, Hans Wilsdorf settled in London,
to work there as a watchmaker. In 1905,
with his brother-in-law, he founded Wilsdorf
& Davis. The two associates specialized in
men's wristwatches, at a time when the
fashion was to carry pocket watches: 'My
personal opinion . . . is that pocket watches
will almost completely disappear and that
wrist watches will replace them definitively!
I am not mistaken in this opinion and you
will see that I am right.'

In 1914, Hans Wilsdorf allegedly changed
the name of the company, which sounded too
German, for one that was easy to pronounce
in all languages: Rolex. A few days before
war broke out, the Rolex watch was the first
to receive a Class A certificate from the
famous Kew Observatory. It was an
immediate success and soldiers, overloaded
with equipment, chose wristwatches in
preference to cumbersome pocket watches.
In 1919, the company moved its headquarters
to Switzerland.

OYSTER, THE FIRST WATERPROOF WRISTWATCH

In 1926, the company made its mark,
revolutionizing modern watchmaking with
the creation of the first waterproof and
dust-resistant watch. Named Oyster, its
case, sealed like a strongbox, guaranteed
optimum protection for the movement. To
announce this feat to the world, Wilsdorf
decided to present a prototype to a young
British swimmer: Mercedes Gleitze. She was
one of the first women to swim across the
English Channel. The crossing lasted
10 hours, and the watch – worn around her

neck – came out of it in perfect working order.
Wilsdorf was ahead of his time when it came
to marketing: he promoted the successful
crossing with the wider public by taking
out a full-page advertisement in the *Daily
Mail*, which showcased the waterproofing of
Rolex watches. To convince sceptics, Wilsdorf
went as far as setting up shop windows and
producing advertising campaigns showing
his watch in an aquarium.

PERPETUAL MOVEMENT

Wilsdorf did not stop there. Despite having
come up with one of the most important
watchmaking inventions of his time, he
spotted a weakness: hand-winding. Adjusting
the time required unscrewing the crown
of the winding mechanism, which created
an opening through which dirt could enter.
In 1931, after years of research, Rolex's
technical teams eventually came up with a
solution: an automatic winding mechanism
with a free rotor, named Perpetual. The
watch rewound itself when it was worn:
every movement of the wearer's wrist
turned the rotor, which engaged with the
mainspring, at the same time guaranteeing
greater accuracy. On the basis of this, over
the decades Rolex has developed a whole
collection of watches, with each new model
fulfilling a specific purpose.

OYSTER PERPETUAL DATEJUST

ROLEX – 1945

In 1945, Rolex launched the first waterproof automatic wristwatch that displayed the date, in an aperture at 3 o'clock: the Datejust. In 1956 there was a further development, with a version that displayed the day and the date: the Day-Date.

MANUFACTURER	ROLEX

1. SEE OPPOSITE

MODEL	OYSTER PERPETUAL DATEJUST 1972
REFERENCE	1601
DIAL	GREY, SIGMA
WINDING MECHANISM	AUTOMATIC
CALIBRE	1570
DIAMETER	36MM
MATERIAL	STEEL, BEZEL IN WHITE GOLD
STRAP	STEEL
TYPE	JUBILEE

2. SEE OVERLEAF, LEFT

MODEL	OYSTER PERPETUAL DAY-DATE 1982
REFERENCE	18038
DIAL	ONYX
WINDING MECHANISM	AUTOMATIC
CALIBRE	3055
DIAMETER	36MM
MATERIAL	GOLD
STRAP	GOLD
TYPE	PRESIDENT

OYSTER PERPETUAL AND HEADS OF STATE

1948	WINSTON CHURCHILL – DATEJUST
1952	DWIGHT D. EISENHOWER – DATEJUST
1962	JOHN F. KENNEDY – DAY-DATE
1963	LYNDON B. JOHNSON – DAY-DATE
1981	RONALD REAGAN – DATEJUST

THE FIRST WATCH TO DISPLAY THE DATE IN AN APERTURE

Rolex celebrated the 40th anniversary of its foundation in 1945 with the launch of the prestigious Oyster Perpetual: a gold Datejust. At its launch it was the first automatic waterproof chronometer wristwatch with a date display in an aperture at 3 o'clock. Although this display is a basic complication today, it was a novelty at the time. Rolex complemented its creation with an innovative five-link strap that fitted the wrist snugly. It featured on other models and was named Jubilee in reference to the anniversary. This watch, recognizable by its ribbed bezel, which had already appeared on some older models, developed further. In 1955, Rolex inserted a magnifying lens in the glass, called Cyclops, which made it easier to read the date, and improved the mechanism. Soon afterwards the watch was made available in steel, and later in the Rolesor version in gold and steel.

A WATCH FOR PRESIDENTS

During World War II, Rolex's production had increased considerably and, at the end of the conflict, it offered watches to notable figures. The 100,000th was given to Winston Churchill in 1948, between his two terms as British prime minister. It was a rose gold Datejust model with a Jubilee strap, and the caseback was engraved with his family's coat of arms. The first US president to own a Rolex was Dwight D. Eisenhower. In 1952, he was given the 150,000th Datejust, ref. 6305, in yellow gold. Five stars – a reference to his military rank as a general – were engraved

on the back, with the initials 'DDE'. John F. Kennedy, whose term began in 1961, refused the watch offered by Rolex. But one model is associated with him: a Day-Date, launched in 1956, the first watch to display, besides the date, the unabbreviated day of the week at the 12 o'clock position on the dial. It was given to him by his mistress Marilyn Monroe. There is a mystery attached to this watch, for the serial number indicates it was made in 1965 – but Kennedy was assassinated two years previously, and Monroe died three years before this. His successor, Lyndon B. Johnson, was the first president officially to wear a yellow-gold Rolex Day-Date. In 1966, Rolex took advantage of this to promote its watch with advertisements that showed the presidential hotline, with the slogan 'The Presidents' watch'. Thus the Day-Date was named the Rolex President. Ronald Reagan continued the tradition with a steel Datejust, but subsequent presidents preferred more modest models.

ROLEX'S CLASSIC RANGE

These models were not specially designed for a sport, a specific environment or a lifestyle. In 1953, the company divided its Oyster range into two categories: the classic models (Datejust and Day-Date) and the professional watches (Submariner and Explorer). The Datejust and Day-Date, the design of which have changed little, are still cornerstones of the Rolex collection.

ROLEX DAY-DATE
REF. 18038, ONYX DIAL

Rolex began to use natural minerals in the 1970s.
Retailers offered their customers unique configurations as
a special order and at an extra cost.

DIALS MADE OF NATURAL MINERALS

FACT SHEET N°6

A feature of modern watchmaking, mineral dials were popularized by Piaget in the second half of the 20th century. They demand a high degree of expertise and, as a result, are only used by prestigious manufacturers.

EXAMPLES OF THE MINERALS USED IN WATCHMAKING

Apart from Piaget, only prestigious manufacturers such as Patek Philippe and Rolex carried out this painstaking work during the 1970s. Rolex retailers offered clients bespoke configurations of the Datejust and Day-Date models at an extra cost.

- **Onyx:** this semi-precious stone is a type of agate and a variety of chalcedony. It is formed in different colours. Rolex only uses the deepest blacks.

- **Lapis lazuli:** an intense blue metamorphic rock that has been used for decorative purposes for 7,000 years. A platinum model was sold for a record £2.3 million ($3 million) at Sotheby's in 2020.

- **Malachite:** a green mineral used for decoration since the late 18th century. The dial of the ref. 4404 Patek Philippe (see page 182) is made from this material and Rolex still uses it today.

- **Tiger's-eye:** a variety of quartz with flashes of brown and yellow. It glows in some dazzling yellow-gold Day-Date models.

There are others, such as pyrite with its dark brilliance, sodalite with its shades of blue (reserved for steel and white gold models) and howlite, which is often confused with marble.

Today, although Piaget is still the benchmark in this area, brands such as Chaumet, Dior and Rolex also offer dials made from coloured stone. Each mineral has a specific quality that gives every piece a unique character – a combination of watchmaking and jewellery.

PIAGET AND ORNAMENTAL MINERALS

Piaget is a Swiss manufacturer founded in 1874 in La Côte-aux-Fées. In Basel in 1957 it unveiled its 2mm thick extra-flat mechanical calibre: the 9P. Three years later it moved the concept forward with the world's thinnest micro-rotor automatic movement: the 12P. Freed from the constraints imposed by thickness, Valentin Piaget, the third generation to be involved in the family business, decided to stand out from the competition with a range of thin, elegant watches, adorned with dials made from semi-precious stones. The use of these minerals – the brand's true signature – revolutionized watchmaking. Boosted by this success, Piaget diversified and launched itself into the world of high-end jewellery – produced alongside its watchmaking business – building a specialist factory in Geneva.

EXPLORER

ROLEX – 1953

In 1953, climbers reached the summit of Mount Everest for the first time.
Hans Wilsdorf, the founder of Rolex, capitalized on this event
with the launch of the Explorer. In 1971, a second version,
aimed at cavers, was launched.

SEE OPPOSITE	**1964 MODEL**
MANUFACTURER	**ROLEX**
MODEL	**EXPLORER I**
REFERENCE	**1016**
DIAL	**LACQUERED (GILT), TROPICAL**
WINDING MECHANISM	**AUTOMATIC**
CALIBRE	**1560**
DIAMETER	**36MM**
MATERIAL	**STEEL**
STRAP	**LEATHER**
TYPE	**SIMPLE**

ROLEX EXPLORER I & II

1952–1953	PRE-EXPLORER 6150
1953–1955	EXPLORER 6350
1955–1959	EXPLORER 6610
1960–1989	EXPLORER 1016
1971–1985	EXPLORER II 1655
1985–1989	EXPLORER II 16550
1989–1999	EXPLORER 14270
1989–2011	EXPLORER II 16570
2001–2010	EXPLORER 114270
2010–2021	EXPLORER 214270
2011–2021	EXPLORER II 216570
2021–	EXPLORER 124270 & EXPLORER II 226570

ROLEX BUBBLE BACK

In 1933, Rolex engineers modified some Oyster models to accommodate the Perpetual movement, which had been patented two years earlier. These watches, which had formerly been hand-wound, became automatic. Rather than designing new cases, the company simply changed the back, widening it to accommodate the new calibres. This thickened back gave these models their name – Bubble Back. They are extremely robust and have been sought after by explorers – especially climbers – since their launch because, among other things, they allow oxygen reserves to be monitored during ascents.

THE HIMALAYAS AS A TEST-BED

During the 1950s, exclusive annual permits were issued for the exploration of the Himalayas and attempts to the summit of Everest. The Swiss obtained theirs in 1952, and were naturally sponsored by Rolex. After battling against the elements, the climbers were forced to abandon their mission a few hundred metres from the summit – despite being accompanied by the Sherpa Tenzing Norgay, who held the altitude record and was on his seventh expedition. In 1953, it was the turn of the British to make the attempt. They were equipped by the measuring instrument manufacturer Smiths. Two teams were formed under the command of Colonel John Hunt; one of these consisted of the New Zealander Sir Edmund Hillary, supported by the now famous Tenzing. On 29 May, at 11.30am, the two men reached the summit. It is not known who attained it first. What is known is that Tenzing wore a Bubble Back, which he had used on his previous expedition, and that Hillary was equipped with a Smiths watch. Realizing the marketing potential, the British company launched a campaign to promote its new Everest range, but it was beaten to it by the advertising genius of Wilsdorf when Rolex launched the ref. 6350. This watch, featuring an iconic 3-6-9 luminous dial, was the first to bear the name Explorer on its dial.

THE BOWELS OF THE EARTH

The Explorer II, ref. 1655, appeared in 1971. It had several special features, as well as a larger diameter (39mm). Designed for cavers, it featured a fourth hand in luminous orange (subsequently sometimes white) pointing towards a fixed bezel and engraved with 24 hours. The aim was to be able to explore in total darkness by immediately differentiating between day and night. Although the orange hand automatically followed the hour hand in the first versions of the watch, from 1985 it could be adjusted separately, endowing the watch with a new GMT function. From that point, the watch was also made in white. When it was launched, the Explorer was not a popular model. Today it is highly sought after and named Freccione – Italian for 'Big Arrow' – a reference to the large arrowhead on the orange hand. When the Freccione changed to white, the watch was known as Albino.

ROLEX EXPLORER II
REF. 1655, CADRAN TIFFANY & CO

A double-signed watch will increase the value considerably.
The Tiffany & Co brand name is certainly the most sought after by collectors.

DOUBLE-SIGNED WATCHES

FACT SHEET N°7

Today, double-signed watches with dials bearing two brand names are highly sought after. Yet at the outset they were simply the result of the commercial strategies of Swiss manufacturers who were keen to get a foothold in certain markets by benefitting from the fame of reputable retailers.

INDICATION OF A WATCH'S PROVENANCE

Before the concept of globalization arrived, watchmaking companies did not necessarily have their own distribution network. Instead, enthusiasts bought their watches from shops that belonged to retailers, some of whom had an even better reputation than the Swiss brands they sold. Consequently, some were allowed to have their name on the dials of the watches alongside that of the manufacturer, which made it easier for the latter to fit into certain markets by taking advantage of the repute of local retailers. Using this strategy, Breitling entered the French market by adding the name LIP, then the world's sixth-biggest watchmaker (see page 108), to some dials. The presence of a retailer's name (or that of a brand, in the case of LIP) on a dial helped to indicate the provenance of a watch, as well as increasing the rarity of a particular model.

MAJOR RETAILERS

All over the world, specialist outlets have contributed to the growth of the biggest watchmaking companies. In London, Asprey, a temple of British luxury, still puts its name on certain models it sells to its global customer base. In Venezuela, the jeweller Serpico y Laino had the exclusive rights to sell Rolex watches until the end of the 1960s. In Rio de Janeiro, Gondolo & Labouriau was the exclusive supplier for Patek Philippe in Brazil (they even issued a special line of watches named Gondolo) from 1872 to 1927. Other big names include Gobbi, a jeweller in Milan, the capital of Italian fashion, and Beyer, Switzerland's oldest specialist watch shop, founded in 1760. Also in Switzerland, Gübelin and Bucherer (which became one of the world's biggest watch retailers) offered watches bearing two names. In France, Hermès distributed Jaeger-LeCoultre and Universal Genève, among others, while Cartier held the sales rights for Audemars Piguet, Patek Philippe and Rolex.

But, in the world of collecting, the most prestigious name to be associated with is certainly that of Tiffany & Co. This famous company was founded in 1837 and its sumptuous flagship store on Fifth Avenue in New York specializes in luxury goods including watches by Rolex, Omega and Patek Philippe. In 1851, a partnership was formed between the latter and the retailer, which was the Stern family's eyes and ears on the American continent. At the end of 2021, to celebrate the 170th anniversary of their collaboration, the ref. 5711 (see page 194) with a sky-blue dial – Tiffany & Co's company colour – was created in a limited edition of 170 watches. A few days later, at an auction organized by Phillips – in New York, naturally – No. 1 sold for a record $6.5 million.

SEAMASTER

OMEGA – 1948

In 1948, Omega celebrated its 100th anniversary with the launch of the Seamaster line. In the process it rooted its reputation in the manufacture of robust, waterproof watches.

SEE OPPOSITE	**1949 MODEL**
MANUFACTURER	**OMEGA**
MODEL	**SEAMASTER**
REFERENCE	**CK 2577**
DIAL	**CREAM, TROPICAL**
WINDING MECHANISM	**AUTOMATIC**
CALIBRE	**351 BUMPER**
DIAMETER	**34MM**
MATERIAL	**STEEL**
STRAP	**METAL**
TYPE	**FIXOFLEX ELASTIC**

OMEGA
CAL. 351 BUMPER

The Bumper first appeared in 1943. Its name refers to the dull sound that can be heard when the rotor strikes a spring.

CREATED FOR THE COMPANY'S 100TH ANNIVERSARY

Omega was founded in 1848 by Louis Brandt. The firm did not adopt its company name until 1897, by which time it had created a calibre of 19 lignes. In the early 20th century, Omega was the first watchmaking brand to be the victim of counterfeit goods. It was the official supplier to the British Royal Air Force, then became a partner of the 1932 Olympic Games in Los Angeles (it is still an Olympic Games partner). Why? Its expertise in robust, waterproof watches. Omega created the Marine for one of the pioneers of modern diving – the French navy officer and inventor Yves Le Prieur. In order to cement its reputation, the Seamaster was launched in 1948, 100 years after the company was founded.

For this model, Omega drew inspiration from World War II submarines – and especially their system of rubber toric joints. Before the advent of these, waterproofing relied on lead or shellac joints, which could be affected by changes in temperature and depth. The Seamaster, with its new system and a specially designed case, was tested down to a depth of 60m and in temperatures fluctuating between -40°C (-40°F) and +50°C (122°F). In order to demonstrate its toughness Omega engineers, who had total faith in their design, attached one to the fuselage of an aeroplane flying the polar route in the winter of 1956. The watch survived the ordeal unscathed.

THE BUMPER MOVEMENT

Not all Seamaster watches display the Seamaster name on their dial. Some, which are believed to have been destined for use by the medical profession, feature a mysterious red hand. Most of the early models have an automatic movement known as Bumper. This name comes from the dull sound the owner can hear while wearing the watch, caused by the rotor striking a spring before reversing its movement. Invented by John Harwood in 1923, and making their first appearance on Omega watches in 1943, these movements feature an oscillating weight that does not rotate through 360 degrees, like a modern rotor, but through 120 degrees. At each end of its motion, springs bounce it back in the opposite direction, thus winding the movement. This simple and effective idea was used during the line's heyday, until the end of the 1950s. The system was fitted to the first Constellation models (see page 60) before being progressively replaced by the 360-degree rotor system, which is more accurate.

OMEGA'S FLAGSHIP MODEL

From its launch, the Seamaster met with a certain success, and became a best seller. It underwent a major overhaul in 1957, with the release of the Seamaster 300 (see page 146), but the classic models, destined for non-professional use, remained in the catalogue. Indeed, the range has never left it. It is still there, in myriad versions, more than 70 years after its creation.

CONSTELLATION

OMEGA – 1952

Aimed at a clientele that valued accuracy and prestige, from its launch in 1952 the Constellation was considered a symbol of watchmaking perfection.

SEE OPPOSITE	1967 MODEL
MANUFACTURER	OMEGA
MODEL	CONSTELLATION TOOL 105 PIE PAN
REFERENCE	168.025
DIAL	SILVER, PIE PAN
WINDING MECHANISM	AUTOMATIC
CALIBRE	564
DIAMETER	34MM
MATERIAL	STEEL
STRAP	LEATHER
TYPE	SIMPLE

**OMEGA
KEW OBSERVATORY ENGRAVING**

On the caseback of each Constellation is an observatory surmounted by eight stars, a reference to the records for accuracy Omega set at the Kew Observatory in London during the 1930s.

ACCURACY AND PRESTIGE

To celebrate its 100th anniversary in 1948, at the same time as the Seamaster (see page 58) Omega launched a limited edition: the Centenary. It was a prestigious gold watch with an automatic movement – a certified chronometer. It was so successful that it immediately sold out. Given the level of enthusiasm, in 1952 Omega created a line that incorporated that model's features: the Constellation. This range was characterized by the refined details used on the watches. The name 'Constellation' appeared on the dials, generally at the 6 o'clock position and above an appliqué star. The caseback was engraved with a medallion depicting an observatory surmounted by eight stars, a reference to the eight records the company achieved in the field of accuracy at the Kew Observatory between 1933 and 1936. The first models featured Bumper movements (see page 58); four years later these were replaced by 360 degree rotors, which were more reliable.

THE PIE PAN DIAL

While it is impossible to list all the variants in the Constellation range, one configuration that was sought after by collectors stood out from the model's launch – the Pie Pan dial. It was given its name because its shape resembled an upturned pie pan; the convex dial had 12 facets and a raised centre. It was used on various versions, notably the Grand Luxe ref. 2699, with a case featuring lyre-shaped lugs (known as dog legs). Until the 1960s, it featured on models of various shapes and made from a range of materials, such as the rare model with a Unicoc case in

super-waterproof steel, ref. 168.025, which required a special tool to be opened. Various textures featured on the dials, such as honeycomb, lacquering and brushing.

A REVOLUTIONARY DESIGN

'At the beginning of the 1960s I discreetly created some models for Omega. I felt a strong connection with that company.' These are the words of the renowned designer Gérald Genta (see page 190). His wife, Évelyne, confirmed that after designing the Polerouter for Universal Genève at the age of 23 (see page 64), her husband worked as an independent designer for Omega. At least two Constellations are attributed to him: ref. 14900 Pie Pan, with onyx markers, and the cushion-shaped ref. 168.009, known as the C-Shape. The Constellation was made in a women's version, and in 1969 broke new ground as the first watch featuring an integrated strap, thanks to a system patented by Pierre Moinat five years earlier. In 1982, Carol Didisheim revolutionized the design with the Manhattan, which had rounded lines. Its bezel featured four prongs designed to retain the sapphire glass for better waterproofing, plus it had a quartz movement. Today, this model is still in the catalogue under the name Constellation, but also Globemaster, a name already used by Omega during the 1950s for the models it sold in the United States.

KONTIKI

ETERNA – 1958

**In 1958, 11 years after the successful Kon-Tiki expedition,
Eterna launched a range of waterproof watches featuring
its patented automatic calibre with ball bearings.**

SEE OPPOSITE	1966 MODEL
MANUFACTURER	ETERNA
MODEL	KONTIKI 20
REFERENCE	130T
DIAL	SILVER
WINDING MECHANISM	AUTOMATIC
CALIBRE	1489K
DIAMETER	37MM
MATERIAL	STEEL
STRAP	LEATHER
TYPE	SIMPLE

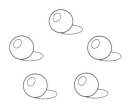

ETERNA
WITH BALL BEARINGS

Eterna owes its reputation
to numerous innovations,
including a rotor mounted
on five ball bearings.

THE 1947 KON-TIKI EXPEDITION

In 1947, the Norwegian anthropologist
Thor Heyerdahl set sail from the port of
Callao, Peru, on board a raft built of balsa
logs (imported from Ecuador), a replica of
traditional pre-Columbian craft. Named Kon-
Tiki (after the Incas' sun god), it had only one
sail and carried the minimum of equipment:
a radio, an inflatable dinghy, survival rations
and waterproof watches. The aim was to
prove to the world that the first Polynesians
were descended from people originating from
South America. The voyage lasted 101 days.
Each crew member wore an Eterna watch,
which Thor Heyerdahl had requested from
the head of the company, Rudolf Schild-
Comtesse. After 8,000 km (4,970 miles), the
voyage ended abruptly on the coral reefs of
Raroia. The crew were in good shape; the
raft less so. As for the watches, they had lost
none of their functions, having withstood
changes in temperature and corrosion from
salt water. In light of this, Eterna launched a
range to celebrate the exploit a decade later –
although Thor Heyerdahl's theory was
still disputed.

1958 – THE ETERNA KONTIKI RANGE

Right from its launch in 1958, the KonTiki
was a commercial success. The steel caseback
features a medallion engraved with an image
of the famous raft. It has a special design:
a dial with oversized, luminous triangles,
containing numerals at 3, 6, 9 and 12 o'clock.
The same year, Eterna launched a more
compact women's model. The KonTiki evolved:
several Super-KonTiki versions were made,
including one featuring a mesh strap

(see page 150). Models that were more classic
in appearence and less like sports watches
also appeared thanks to the KonTiki 20
range; some of these watches featured indexes
in semiprecious stones. Today, the KonTiki
continues to fulfil its promise. In 2006,
Olav Heyerdahl wore a modern one when he
set out to replicate his grandfather's feat.

FIVE BALL BEARINGS

In 1948, five ball bearings prepared the
ground for Eterna's world renown. From
then on, they also formed the logo of
this manufacturer from Granges. At the
time, many manufacturers refused to use
automatic movements as it would make their
watches thicker. Moreover, the first rotor
movements were especially prone to wear,
friction and breakage. Eterna invented a
solution: an automatic movement with a
system of low-friction ball bearings, each
with a diameter of 0.65mm, which cushioned
it from shocks and thus facilitated the
functioning of the oscillating weight. With
the development of this movement, Eterna
set a standard for automatic calibres.

POLEROUTER

UNIVERSAL GENÈVE – 1954

In 1954, Universal Genève created the Polerouter to commemorate the SAS airline's first commercial flight over the North Pole. It was resistant to magnetic fields and featured a micro-rotor.

SEE OPPOSITE	**1967 MODEL**
MANUFACTURER	**UNIVERSAL GENÈVE**
MODEL	**POLEROUTER DE LUXE**
REFERENCE	**10357**
DIAL	**BLACK, STARDUST**
WINDING MECHANISM	**AUTOMATIC**
CALIBRE	**215 MICRO-ROTOR**
DIAMETER	**35MM**
MATERIAL	**GOLD**
STRAP	**LEATHER**
TYPE	**SIMPLE**

UNIVERSAL GENÈVE
CAL. 215 MICRO-ROTOR

The micro-rotor differs from other types in its shape, size and position: it is a reduced size semicircle integrated within the movement.

THE SAS'S EXPLOIT

An experimental DC-6B aircraft belonging to the Scandinavian Airlines System (SAS) successfully connected Los Angeles with Copenhagen by taking routes over the Arctic in 1952. Just two years later, on 15 November, the first commercial flight over the North Pole took place; journalists and the prime ministers of Norway, Denmark and Sweden were on board. The flight lasted 27 hours and 15 minutes, with a three-hour refuelling stop in Winnipeg, Canada.

To commemorate its feat and equip its pilots, SAS turned to its official supplier, then a specialist in chronographs (see page 84), to create a model that could withstand the extreme magnetic fields at the poles, which tend to compromise the accuracy of navigation and timekeeping instruments. Universal Genève was eager to take on the task and attach its name to the exploit, just as Rolex had done with the ascent of Mount Everest (see page 54). The company created the Polerouter model – initially named Polarouter – after calling on young designer Gérald Genta (see page 190).

GÉRALD GENTA STARTS TO MAKE HIS MARK

Aged 23 at the time, the future creator of the Royal Oak and the Nautilus left his mark on this model. Besides its antimagnetic properties, it was the Polerouter's visual appeal that was celebrated by watchmaking enthusiasts. While many variants exist, the lyre-shaped lugs (which also feature on some Speedmasters – see page 98),

as well as an internal bezel divided into five-minute segments, shaped the character of these functional watches.

MICRO-ROTOR SYSTEM

Under the bonnet of the early versions is a Bumper movement (see page 58). But the chief point of interest in these models is the movement that was fitted to them during the mid-1950s: the micro-rotor that both Universal Genève and Büren claim to have invented. A true watchmaking work of art, the micro-rotor rewinds automatic movements, but differs from traditional rotors in size, shape and position. The oscillating weight is normally a flat semicircle that sits over the movement. Here, the micro-rotor is a small semicircle that fits within it. The latter's reduced size is why the Polerouter is thin for an automatic watch of its time.

Following the Polerouter's commercial success, Universal Genève launched several models under its name, including luxury gold versions and dive watches, some featuring the Super Compressor case (see page 148).

EL PRIMERO

ZENITH – 1969

**On 10 January 1969, after seven years of development,
the first automatic chronograph movement, the El Primero calibre,
was launched at a press conference held in its honour.**

SEE OPPOSITE	1969 MODEL
MANUFACTURER	ZENITH
MODEL	EL PRIMERO
REFERENCE	A386
DIAL	SILVER-PLATED, COLOURED SUBDIALS
WINDING MECHANISM	AUTOMATIC
CALIBRE	3019 PHC
DIAMETER	38MM
MATERIAL	STEEL
STRAP	LEATHER
TYPE	SIMPLE

ZENITH
CAL. 3019 PHC

The first automatic chronograph movement, the El Primero calibre was unveiled by the world's press on 10 January 1969, a few months before it was shown in Basel.

1962 – BIRTH OF A CHALLENGE

Chronographs were extremely popular during the 1960s. The Lemania 321 calibre proved its worth for Omega (see page 101), as did the Valjoux 72 for Rolex and other manufacturers (see page 79). There were more, but they were all hand-wound. In 1962, Zenith, which was founded in 1865, set itself the challenge of developing a chronograph with an integrated automatic winding mechanism to celebrate its centenary three years' later. It drew up a specification: it must be automatic, thin (6.5mm), with a 50-hour power reserve and an escapement with a column wheel. A few months before the planned launch, Zenith also opted for high frequency (5Hz), anticipating the advent of a new technology: quartz (see page 209). The calibre's code name was 3019 PHC.

1969 – LAUNCH OF EL PRIMERO

As the specification for this innovative movement expanded, what was meant to take three years ended up taking seven. The company put back the launch in order to offer a state of the art calibre. In 1968, the matter took on more urgency when Zenith heard that Breitling had a competing project in association with Hamilton-Büren, Dubois Dépraz and Heuer-Leonidas (see page 94) – the calibre 11.

The first prototypes were finalized at the end of 1968, and the calibre was unveiled to the world's press on 10 January 1969, under the name El Primero and with the reference A384. Gold and steel versions were exhibited a few months later in Basel. It featured a date at 4.30 and a red second hand with a rectangular tip. The movement, and the

design of the different variants that featured it – especially the reference A386 with three-tone dials – was immediately acclaimed.

THE QUARTZ CRISIS AND THE REBIRTH OF THE CALIBRE

During the 1970s, watches fitted with a quartz movement became more popular than mechanical watches. Zenith did not escape this trend, and in 1975 a turning point was reached: the Americans, who had owned the company since the end of the 1970s, decided to stop manufacturing mechanical watches and ordered the disposal of the relevant tools. One company employee, Charles Vermot, who had been in charge of the manufacture of *ébauches* for 40 years, opposed this, stating: 'Without discounting progress, I note that the world is like this; there are always backtracks. You are wrong to believe in the total stoppage of the automatic mechanical chronograph as well. I am convinced that one day your company will be able to benefit from the fads and fashions that the world has always known.' In the utmost secrecy, he hid the plans and tools for making calibres in the factory's attic.

In 1978, the Americans sold the brand to some Swiss shareholders. At the beginning of the 1980s, Charles Vermot's words rang true when mechanical watches came back into fashion. Ebel was looking for an automatic chronograph movement and approached Zenith, hoping to use the last movements that had not been destroyed. Then, Rolex, which was in search of an automatic movement for its Daytona chronograph, also called on the company. The treasures of the past were taken out of their hiding place and production was successfully restarted.

CHRONOGRAPHS

CHAPTER 2

CHRONOGRAPHS

MOTOR SPORT

From the 1960s onwards, watchmaking and motor racing became inextricably linked, with the appearance of legendary chronographs and iconic races.

THE HEUER REVOLUTION

In 2013, Jean-Marie Schaller, CEO of Les Ateliers Louis Moinet, revealed a major discovery to the world: the first ever chronograph, which had lain hidden for 150 years at the home of a noble French family. In 1816, like many of his contemporaries, Louis Moinet was on a quest for accuracy. And he attained his goal: his creation was accurate to one-sixtieth of a second, or 216,000 vibrations per hour. At the time, it was rare to be able to measure one-fifth of a second, although in some cases one-tenth was achieved. A century would go by before Heuer exceeded this frequency, reaching 360,000 vibrations. This technical innovation changed the history of motor racing by allowing drivers to measure, and gain, precious time.

CARS AND WATCHMAKING

Thanks to this revolutionary technology, Heuer became the official timekeeper at major sporting events. Before it sold wristwatches, the company manufactured on-board instruments for cars, such as the Montecarlo and the Autavia (see page 92), that facilitated timekeeping during races. From 1962, with the launch of his wrist chronograph Autavia, followed by the Carrera (see page 88) and Monaco (see page 94) models, Jack Heuer firmly established himself in the sector.

Motor racing is generally synonymous with speed. A tachymeter scale is thus designed to measure the speed of an object over a given distance. In 1957, the Speedmaster model revolutionized the genre by placing it on an engraved steel bezel (see page 98). Before it was sent into space, the Speedmaster and its calibre 321 were aimed at racing drivers.

In 1963, Rolex launched its new chronograph, the Cosmograph, ref. 6239. In contrast to the previous reference (ref. 6238), the scale was engraved on an external bezel (as with the Omega Speedmaster, launched six years earlier) and – a new feature for a chronograph at that time – the subdials were in a colour that contrasted with the rest of the dial for improved readability. People spoke of Panda or Reverse Panda dials, with black subdials on a white background or vice versa (see page 126).

Other watch manufacturers targeted this market, such as Enicar, with its Sherpa Graph model (see page 82); Tudor, Rolex's younger sibling, with the Homeplate (see page 80); and, of course, Universal Genève, a specialist in the field (see page 84).

SPECIAL FEATURES OF A MOTOR RACING WATCH

Specific characteristics set aside motor racing watches from the rest. First of all, these are chronographs with two or three counters, endowed with a complementary mechanism that allows the measurement and display of elapsed times. This complication demands sophisticated construction, especially in its most noble form: the column wheel chronograph, such as the 321 calibres (see page 101) and the Valjoux 72 calibres (see page 79).

Moreover, these watches feature a tachymeter bezel for calculating speed. To use this, all that is required is to start the chronograph when passing a kilometre marker and to stop it when passing the next. The time the vehicle has taken to cover the kilometre makes it possible to calculate its speed in kilometres per hour.

Also, such watches must have a contrasting dial, allowing them to be read at high speed. This may be a Panda dial, but could also be coloured. Models from the time include exotic versions.

Finally, motor racing watches often come with a Rallye-type strap in leather or rubber, which is both breathable and comfortable (see pages 90 and 91).

COSMOGRAPH DAYTONA 'PAUL NEWMAN'

ROLEX – 1963

Launched in 1963, the Rolex Cosmograph Daytona, made famous by the actor Paul Newman, is a professional watch originally designed for racing drivers.

MANUFACTURER	ROLEX
WINDING MECHANISM	MECHANICAL

1. SEE OPPOSITE

MODEL	DAYTONA PAUL NEWMAN 1968
REFERENCE	6239
DIAL	EXOTIC
CALIBRE	722 – VALJOUX 72
DIAMETER	36MM
MATERIAL	STEEL

2. SEE OVERLEAF, LEFT

MODEL	DAYTONA PAUL NEWMAN DIAL 1968
REFERENCE	6239
DIAL	EXOTIC
CALIBRE	722 – VALJOUX 72
DIAMETER	36MM
MATERIAL	STEEL

3. SEE OVERLEAF, RIGHT

MODEL	DAYTONA 1979
REFERENCE	6265
DIAL	GOLD
CALIBRE	727 – VALJOUX 72
DIAMETER	37.5MM
MATERIAL	GOLD

WORLD RECORD

At its launch, the Daytona delighted racing drivers, including the actor Paul Newman, who contributed to its high profile with the general public. The exotic dials were nicknamed Paul Newman. In 2017, his personal watch, ref. 6239, broke all records when it sold for £14 million ($17.8 million) at Phillips in 15 minutes.

DAYTONA INTERNATIONAL SPEEDWAY

At the beginning of the last century Daytona, an American seaside town, attracted motor-sport lovers because it was home to a track on the beach. In 1935 the British racing driver Malcolm Campbell beat all land records there at the wheel of his Bluebird, with a Rolex Oyster on his wrist. The tradition of motor racing endured there with the inauguration of a permanent racing circuit – the Daytona International Speedway – in 1959. It hosted a prestigious endurance race, which was sponsored by Rolex. In 1963 the manufacturer launched its ref. 6239 Cosmograph, which did not yet bear the name Daytona, although it was presented as a prize to winning drivers. In the first catalogues it featured under the name 'Le Mans'. It was only in around 1965 that the name Daytona appeared on the dial, a reference to the partnership with the famous race, which is still held and is today often referred to as The Rolex Race.

PERPETUAL EVOLUTION

During the 1930s, Rolex earned an enduring reputation for sports watches thanks to its Oyster case. Some 20 years later, the manufacturer aimed to enter the chronograph market and called on Valjoux to equip its watches (see page 79). The ancestor of the Daytona is undeniably the ref. 6234, with an internal telemetry scale used to calculate distance. The ref. 6238 that followed it is unquestionably regarded as a pre-Daytona model. It was available until 1967, and features baton hands and

an internal scale – a tachymeter scale this time used to calculate speed. The ref. 6239, which dates from 1963, is considered to be the first true Daytona, despite the absence of the name on the dial. It stands out initially for its external bezel, engraved with a tachymeter scale, and its two-tone, Panda-type design (see page 126), which was designed to improve readability. In 1965, when the Daytona name began to feature and exotic dials appeared, the model evolved with ref. 6240, which introduced screw push-buttons and a bezel with a black insert. More references followed, featuring either a metal bezel or a black one, screw or round push-buttons, and a variety of dials. The last, ref. 6263 (black bezel) and 6265 (metal bezel), with screw push-buttons, were available until 1987 in either steel or gold versions. The main change in the Daytona appeared in 1988: the 16500 series, available in three colours (steel, gold and steel, and gold) now had a diameter of 40mm instead of 36mm, a sapphire glass in place of Plexiglas and – a great novelty – an automatic rather than mechanical movement, based on the Zenith El Primero calibre (see page 66). It featured in Daytona watches until the 2000s, when Rolex began to make its own movement, the calibre 4130. The final notable development concerned the look of the watch: the bezel was now made from Cerachrom, a material that is less likely to become scratched.

ENGRAVED HEIRLOOMS

FACT SHEET N°8

Although Reverso owners are still offered the option of having the hinged case engraved, this practice is increasingly rare today. However, it allows a watch to be transformed into an heirloom for future generations.

Marlon Brando and the Rolex GMT:

'M. Brando'

Marlon Brando owned several engraved watches, three of which are famous. At the beginning of his career he wore a Rolex Oyster (see page 48). A present from his parents for his 19th birthday, it bore the inscription: *'To Bud from Mother & Dad 1943'*. After he starred in *The Godfather* in 1972, the actor was given a Datejust with the engraving *'Vito's'*. But the most famous was certainly his Rolex GMT, which he wore in *Apocalypse Now* in 1979. During filming Francis Ford Coppola asked Brando to remove it. The latter refused, explaining that if viewers looked at his watch it was because he was not doing his job properly. After a long discussion the Rolex stayed, but without the Pepsi bezel, on the pretext that it better fitted his character, Colonel Kurtz.

Richard Nixon and the Omega Speedmaster:

'Richard M. Nixon, President of the United States, to mark man's conquest of space with time, through time, on time'

After Apollo 11 landed on the moon in 1969, US President Richard M. Nixon was given a gold Speedmaster (see page 98), one of a limited edition of 1,014, bearing a special engraving. Because of its great value, he was obliged to refuse the watch, which can now be seen at the Omega museum in Bienne. Fifty years later, the Swiss company relaunched the model to commemorate the historic event.

John F. Kennedy and the Rolex Day-Date:

'JACK With love as always from MARILYN May 29th 1962'

History relates that Marilyn Monroe gave JFK a Rolex Day-Date on 29 May 1962, his birthday and the day she famously sang *Happy Birthday, Mr President*. However, he was never seen or photographed wearing it. According to legend, he got rid of it with the help of his assistants. Later, it reappeared at auction but there was a problem – its serial number indicates it was made in 1965, two years after he was assassinated. QED.

Jackie Kennedy and the Cartier Tank:

'Stas to Jackie 23 Feb. 63. 2:05 AM to 9:35 PM'

In 1963, Jackie Kennedy was given a Cartier Tank (see page 34) by her brother-in-law, Prince Stanislaw 'Stas' Radziwill. The engraving commemorates an 80-km (50-mile) walk undertaken by the family, even though Jackie and JFK did not cover the whole distance.

John Landis and the Cartier Tank:

'Fuck'em if they can't take a joke'

John Landis was a cult director in the 1980s whose fims included *The Blues Brothers*. There is no date, no recipient is mentioned and no precise explanation for this humorous engraving, which fits his personality. All that is known is that the watch was given to one of his producers.

DRIVE CAREFULLY ME

Fittingly, the most famous engraving appears on the most famous watch: Paul Newman's Rolex Daytona. It recently set a record price of £14 million ($17.8 million) at auction, and was photographed for the cover of this book. The actor liked to drive fast. His wife, Joanne, knew this. 'Drive Carefully Me' is thus an appeal to prudence from a woman in love with her husband. It should be noted that the actor owned two other Daytona models, also gifts from his wife. One was engraved with 'Drive Slowly – Joanne', and the other with 'Drive Very Slowly – Joanne'.

ROLEX DAY-DATE
JOHN F. KENNEDY

OMEGA SPEEDMASTER
RICHARD NIXON

CARTIER TANK
JOHN LANDIS

CARTIER TANK
JACKIE KENNEDY

ROLEX GMT
MARLON BRANDO

ROLEX DAYTONA
PAUL NEWMAN

COSMOGRAPH DAYTONA 'PAUL NEWMAN'
REF. 6239; 722 VALJOUX 72

The Daytona watches of the time were fitted with modified Valjoux 72 column wheel movements.
The 722 benefited from a balance with adjustable inertia, thanks to its pair of Microstella
screws on the balance wheel.

VALJOUX MOVEMENTS

FACT SHEET N°9

**Valjoux specializes in making *ébauches* for chronograph movements.
These incomplete movements, which are not assembled, are sold to watchmaking companies
who then incorporate them in their watches.**

Valjoux was founded in Bioux, in the Joux valley, in 1901. It was originally run by brothers John and Charles Reymond. At the end of the 19th century, at the age of around 20, they devoted themselves to watchmaking and worked for Auguste Rochat-Benoît. Dissatisfied with the quality of the movements they were working on, they decided to develop their own. The brothers then set up their company, Reymond Frères SA, and raised the funds to buy the L'Abbaye factory, which specialized in watchmaking.

In 1914, Reymond Frères SA launched the calibre 22, a chronograph movement with two counters, which was reduced in size to meet the demand for smaller watches, with the calibre 23, in 1916. In 1929, John Reymond's sons, Marius and Arnold, took over the company, which then became Valjoux SA. World War I saw a pause in its development, but growth resumed after the war and the factory continued to expand. Valjoux earned the confidence of prestigious manufacturers, delivering to companies such as Rolex, Patek Philippe and Universal Genève. In around 1938, before joining Ébauches SA and then being taken over by ETA Manufacture, Valjoux launched a new family

of chronograph movements based on the calibre 23, this time with three counters: the calibre 72.

THE VALJOUX FAMILY 23/72

The Valjoux 23 and 72, which were manufactured for more than 60 years, were among the most sought-after movements, and featured a column wheel. This toothed component co-ordinates the phases of the chronograph's function: start, stop and return to zero of the chronograph hand. In modern high-quality chronographs the wheel is replaced by a system of cams. Initially featuring one push-button, the Valjoux 23 family with two counters was fitted to the first chronographs with two push-buttons created by Willy Breitling in the mid-1930s. The group includes several complications, including the Flyback (230), Date (232) and even the Triple Date (23C). The 23 calibres are basically Valjoux 72 calibres with three counters, which use certain identical components. The Valjoux 72 family also contains various complications, including the Triple Date (72C) and Triple Date with phases of the moon (88) – the jewel in the company's crown. At Rolex, the variant of the

Valjoux 72 was initially designated 72B (it contained a Breguet spiral and Microstella screws on the balancer). Later versions were designated 722, 722-1 and 727.

HIGHLY SOUGHT-AFTER ORIGINAL MOVEMENTS

Production of the original Valjoux 23/72 movements ended in around 1974, when the company began to manufacture the 7736 calibres with cams in large numbers. Production of the prestigious column-wheel movements did not stop however, for the later versions 236 (of the 23) and 726 (of the 72) were used for a short time during the 1970s. Today these movements are highly sought-after and fitted to limited edition watches, but valued by watchmakers as spare parts.

HOMEPLATE

TUDOR – 1970

The first chronograph from the Tudor brand, Rolex's younger sibling, appeared in 1970. Called the Oysterdate, it was named Homeplate thanks to the shape of its markers.

SEE OPPOSITE	**1971 MODEL**

MANUFACTURER	**TUDOR**
MODEL	**OYSTERDATE HOMEPLATE**
REFERENCE	**7031**

DIAL	**GREY, COLOURED, HOMEPLATE**
WINDING MECHANISM	**MECHANICAL**
CALIBRE	**VALJOUX 7734**
DIAMETER	**39MM**

MATERIAL	**STEEL**
STRAP	**STEEL**
TYPE	**OYSTER**

HOMEPLATE

1970	•	HOMEPLATE 7000
1971	•	MONTECARLO 7100
1976	•	BIG BLOCK 9400
1989	•	BIG BLOCK 79100

1970 – THE FIRST TUDOR CHRONOGRAPH

Rolex and Tudor are closely linked. The latter, with a trademark registered in 1926, is considered the former's younger sibling. Hans Wilsdorf's words, on founding the Montres Tudor SA company in 1946, convey this: 'For several years I have been studying the possibility of making a watch that our dealers can sell at a lower price than our Rolex watches, and which is worthy of the same confidence.' The Oyster Prince model was launched in 1952, followed two years later by a line of dive watches. However, it was not until the beginning of the 1970s that a chronograph – the series 7000 Oysterdate – was launched (a shield logo replaced the rose the company had previously used).

TWO ICONIC LINES

Waterproof to a depth of 50m, thanks to Oyster cases and screw push-buttons, and driven by Valjoux 7734 calibres with cams (see page 79), the first Oysterdates were bigger than was usual at the time (39mm). The pronounced angle of the lugs was a characteristic, but it was the very graphic style of the dial that delighted buyers. These featured unusual painted pentagon-shaped markers, which earned the watch the name Homeplate, because they were reminiscent of the shape of the first base on a baseball pitch. There are three versions – two that went into production and one prototype – which differ on account of their bezels. The 7031/0 has a bezel surmounted by a black disc with a tachymeter scale; the 7032/0 features a steel bezel engraved with a tachymeter scale; and the third, the 7033/0, has a revolving bi-directional bezel with a black disc calibrated with 12 units. A year later, and until 1977, a new 7100 series was produced, and named Montecarlo on account of its dials that resembled roulette wheels. It retained the look of the previous models, even though a blue variant was introduced. This second generation used the same case as the previous one, but the movement was changed: in place of the Valjoux 7734 with cams, a Valjoux 234 with a column wheel, which was more accurate, was used.

LAST GENERATIONS

Significant evolution occurred in 1976, when, in its third series, Tudor decided to use an automatic movement (the Valjoux 7750, which competed with El Primero, see page 66), 12 years earlier than Rolex, its elder sibling, fitted one to the Daytona. Named Prince Oysterdate, the cases were thicker in order to make room for the rotor of the new movement. This series, the 9400, is referred to as Big Block. The name also applies to the 79100 series, which appeared in 1989 and featured only minimal modifications. Again, the differences betwen the watches are their bezels and several versions of the dial which were graphic or of the Panda-type (see page 126). From 1996, and with the reference 79200, the company made its case thinner. The new era of the Tudor chronograph began in 2017, with the launch of the Black Bay, fitted with a movement manufactured in collaboration with Breitling.

SHERPA GRAPH

ENICAR – 1960

**The Sherpa range was created following a mountaineering expedition
where the members were equipped with an Enicar. Its models include
a chronograph that is much appreciated by racing drivers.**

SEE OPPOSITE	**1965 MODEL**
MANUFACTURER	**ENICAR**
MODEL	**SHERPA GRAPH**
REFERENCE	**MARK II**
DIAL	**BLACK, SILVER SUBDIALS, BLUE TACHYMETER SCALE**
WINDING MECHANISM	**MECHANICAL**
CALIBRE	**VALJOUX 72**
DIAMETER	**40MM**
MATERIAL	**STEEL**
STRAP	**LEATHER**
TYPE	**SIMPLE**

ENICAR WATCH Co.
4 — 8 2

ENICAR
BAYONET CASE

Each of these watches has a
waterproof bayonet case, developed
with Ervin Piquerez SA (EPSA).
Inside the caseback is the company
logo: a deep-sea diver.

THE SHERPA RANGE

The Racine family, which was based in
Granges, Switzerland, made its name in
watchmaking in the mid-19th century. In
1914, its founder Ariste Racine reversed
the letters of his surname and registered
the name Enicar. His son, Ariste Junior,
succeeded him in 1938. From the 1950s
onwards, he brought new inspiration to the
company, orientating it towards products
designed for adventure. At the same time
the logo representing Saturn, the master
of time in Roman mythology, appeared.
Enicar also attracted attention when it
invented Ultrasonic, a technique for cleaning
mechanisms using ultrasound, which gave
rise to a model of the same name. But it
was a historic event on 18 May 1956 that
truly established the company, when Lhotse
and Mount Everest were conquered by
expeditions whose members were equipped
with waterproof Enicars. The manufacturer
was suddenly front-page news, and a few
months later took advantage of this publicity
by creating the Sherpa range and its
variations.

SHERPA GRAPH

In 1960, Enicar unveiled its Sherpa Graph.
Based on a Valjoux 72 (see page 79), this
model was very popular with racing drivers.
At its launch, a brochure introduced the
chronograph with the words of the Formula 1
driver Stirling Moss: 'The Enicar Sherpa
is definitely the watch I have always wanted.'
During that decade several versions
appeared, displaying subtle differences
(MK I, II, III and IV). These references
featured three counters and a large diameter

for the time: 40mm. Dials of various
colours and hands of various shapes were
used, but the versions all shared a Super
Compressor-type bayonet case (see page 148)
manufactured exclusively for Enicar by Ervin
Piquerez SA (EPSA) .

SHERPA AND GRAPH VARIANTS

As indicated above, the Sherpa range is
extremely broad. Watches designed for
different uses are contained within the same
series. They are categorized by the number of
crowns they have. Models with a single crown
are dive watches, such as the Sherpa Diver
and GMT. Those with two include, notably,
a professional dive version named Super
Dive, but also a completely new line aimed at
racing drivers – the Guide, a wide GMT-type
watch with an external bezel (see page 164),
and the Super Jet, with an internal bezel.
Even though they are not part of the Sherpa
range, it is important to mention three other
watches from Enicar's Graph range. They
too are fitted with the famous Valjoux 72,
and benefit from an external bezel, a great
novelty compared to the Sherpa Graph: the
Aquagraph, for professional divers; the Jet
Graph, for pilots; and the less common Super
Graph, whose bezel is inversely calibrated
from 60 to 0 minutes, for more general use.

COMPAX 'NINA RINDT'

UNIVERSAL GENÈVE – 1936

**From the 1930s onwards Universal Genève specialized
in chronographs. The Compax series appeared in 1936 and,
until the 1970s, it went through many variations.**

MANUFACTURER	UNIVERSAL GENÈVE

1. SEE OPPOSITE

MODEL	COMPAX 'NINA RINDT' 1964
REFERENCE	885103/02
DIAL	WHITE PANDA, TROPICAL
WINDING MECHANISM	MECHANICAL
CALIBRE	VALJOUX 72
DIAMETER	36MM
MATERIAL	STEEL
STRAP	LEATHER
TYPE	SIMPLE

2. SEE OVERLEAF, LEFT

MODEL	COMPAX 'EVIL NINA' 1965
REFERENCE	885103/01
DIAL	BLACK REVERSE PANDA
WINDING MECHANISM	MECHANICAL
CALIBRE	VALJOUX 72
DIAMETER	36MM
MATERIAL	STEEL
STRAP	LEATHER
TYPE	SIMPLE

3. SEE OVERLEAF, RIGHT

MODEL	COMPAX 'EXOTIC NINA' 1965
REFERENCE	885107
DIAL	EXOTIC BLUE
WINDING MECHANISM	MECHANICAL
CALIBRE	VALJOUX 72
DIAMETER	36MM
MATERIAL	STEEL
STRAP	LEATHER
TYPE	SIMPLE

UNIVERSAL GENÈVE

In 1894, the Descombes et Perret company – named after the two young associates who founded it – was formed in Neuchâtel, Switzerland. The Universal Watch brand name was registered, but the company was content with making dials, cases and other components. Nevertheless, that same year it registered a patent for an ambitious watch with a 24-hour display and jump hour. The premature death of Descombes in 1897 disrupted the company's plans, and led Perret to find a new associate, Berthoud. The Perret & Berthoud company took over the brand and specialized in manufacturing watches with complications (see page 159). In 1917, the first chronograph was unveiled – a wristwatch featuring a calibre of 17 lignes. In 1919, the company moved its headquarters to Geneva in order to be close to the business centre of Swiss watchmaking.

THE ART OF CHRONOGRAPHS

Highly prized in literary and artistic circles after World War I, Universal Genève watches became firmly established during the 1920s. Its subtle women's collections, and the option of personalizing each model, earned the manufacturer the moniker 'the couturier of watches'. As if to prove this, some 10 years later Universal collaborated with the Hermès fashion house, which distributed its products, launching a Compax chronograph bearing both brand names. This series is one of the most iconic watches in the history of watchmaking. Launched in 1936, two years after the Compur, it offered many variants, such as the Aero-Compax and the Uni-Compax, but most notably the Tri-Compax,

launched in 1944 for the company's 50th anniversary (see page 178). Available in a variety of configurations, the steel models, of the tool watch type, generally feature luminous hands; the gold models, which are more formal and elegant, feature blued-steel hands.

THE ICONIC NINA RINDT

Among collectors it is not unusual for the name of a celebrity to be associated with a watch model – for example, the Monaco Steve McQueen or the Daytona Paul Newman. Universal Genève's Compax ref. 885103, produced from 1964 to 1967, can be confused with the latter, especially the ref. 6241, for they have similar features: a Panda dial, a tachymeter bezel, round push-buttons, a diameter of 36mm and a Valjoux 72 calibre (see page 79). This reference is called Nina Rindt because the famous 1960s model, Nina Lincoln, wife of the Formula 1 world champion Jochen Rindt, wore this watch. Photographs show her timing her husband, or waiting in the paddocks, with this watch with a bund strap (see page 74) on her wrist. The existing variants of this watch are named according to their features. Thus the black version with red hands is dubbed Evil Nina, while the one with an exotic dial is Exotic Nina.

CARRERA

HEUER – 1963

Created on the initiative of Jack Heuer, the Carrera is worn in motor races as much as in conference halls. In the history of watchmaking, it is a cult chronograph.

MANUFACTURER	HEUER

1. SEE OPPOSITE

MODEL	CARRERA 1964
REFERENCE	2447D (DECIMAL BEZEL)
DIAL	SILVER
WINDING MECHANISM	MECHANICAL
CALIBRE	VALJOUX 72
DIAMETER	36MM
MATERIAL	STEEL
STRAP	LEATHER
TYPE	SIMPLE

2. SEE OVERLEAF, LEFT

MODEL	CARRERA DATO 12 1966
REFERENCE	3147S (SILVER), FIRST ONE MADE
DIAL	SILVER
WINDING MECHANISM	MECHANICAL
CALIBRE	LANDERON 189
DIAMETER	36MM
MATERIAL	STEEL
STRAP	LEATHER
TYPE	RALLYE

3. SEE OVERLEAF, RIGHT

MODEL	CARRERA DATO 45 DE 1968
REFERENCE	3147N (BLACK) 2E EX.
DIAL	BLACK, DATO WHITE
WINDING MECHANISM	MECHANICAL
CALIBRE	LANDERON 189
DIAMETER	36MM
MATERIAL	STEEL
STRAP	LEATHER
TYPE	RALLYE

JACK HEUER, ENTREPRENEUR

Édouard Heuer founded The Heuer Watch Company in 1860 at Saint-Imier, Switzerland. In 1887, it patented a mechanism with an oscillating pinion that made it possible to manufacture the accurate, simplified chronometers popular since the end of the 19th century. In 1916, demand grew following the launch of the Mikrograph, developed by the founder's son, which could measure elapsed time down to 1/100th of a second. Some 20 years later, a partnership with Abercrombie & Fitch, which at the time specialized in hiking equipment, saw the arrival of an invention that marked a turning point for the company. The head of the brand asked Heuer to make him a watch that could predict the tides: the Maréographe. Although the technical challenge was hard, the founder's 15-year-old great-grandson, Jack, thought his science teacher would be able to design such an instrument. This initiative allowed him to be invited into the creative process and to play a role within the company. In 1959, he moved to the United States and took charge of the company's American operation. Three years later, on learning that his uncle wanted to sell, he returned to Switzerland to buy his shares and became a majority shareholder.

BIRTH OF THE CARRERA

In 1962, a year after the launch of the Autavia wristwatch (see page 92), Heuer unveiled the Carrera. The name was a reference to the Carrera Panamericana, a legendary motor race held in Mexico. The first generations of this watch were notable for their readability: their very refined dials were available in black or silver, and were mounted in 36mm cases made by Piquerez (see page 148) with Valjoux calibres, or Landeron calibres in the case of certain rare references with a date. Jack Heuer especially admired the work of the modernist designers Oscar Niemeyer, Charles Eames and Le Corbusier, and applied their principles to the watch, creating a model that was functional and stripped of superfluities.

EVOLUTION AND RENAISSANCE

In 1969 (with Breitling and Hamilton-Büren), Heuer registered a patent for the development of an automatic chronograph movement named Chrono-Matic 11 (see page 94). It was fitted to three models in the catalogue, including the Monaco and the Carrera. For technical reasons to do with the calibre, the crowns were located on the left. Heuer forestalled all criticism by explaining that the crown no longer served any purpose – as the watch was automatic there was no need to touch it. To accommodate this new movement, the design was changed and cases became barrel-shaped. During the 1970s, the model's golden age, partnerships were formed with racing drivers or teams, and there were many variants. But despite its success the line did not survive the quartz crisis (see page 209). The company was sold in 1982, and the line was then removed from the catalogue. In 1985, Heuer was bought by Techniques d'Avant-Garde (TAG), which also owned the McLaren Formula 1 team. For the relaunch of the Carrera in 1996 at Monza, the TAG group asked Jack Heuer to present this watch.

AUTAVIA

HEUER – 1962

A portmanteau word formed from 'automobile' and 'aviation', the Autavia chronograph appeared in 1962. This designation had already been used during the 1930s for on-board instruments.

SEE OPPOSITE	1968 MODEL
MANUFACTURER	HEUER
MODEL	AUTAVIA
REFERENCE	2446C (COMPRESSOR)
DIAL	REVERSE PANDA
WINDING MECHANISM	MECHANICAL
CALIBRE	VALJOUX 72
DIAMETER	40MM
MATERIAL	STEEL
STRAP	LEATHER
TYPE	RALLYE

AUTAVIA

1930s	AUTAVIA ON-BOARD INSTRUMENT
1962	HEUER AUTAVIA
1968	HEUER AUTAVIA COMPRESSOR
1969	HEUER AUTAVIA CHRONOMATIC

THE ORIGIN OF THE NAME

The origin of the name Autavia goes back to the 1930s, when Heuer designed on-board instruments for racing cars and aircraft. A portmanteau word formed from the words 'automobile' and 'aviation', a reference to the two key sectors where the company operated, the model was replaced soon afterwards by the Montecarlo, which was more readable. However, it was out of the question for the company to drop such a striking name. Three decades later the Autavia was resurrected through a new creation by Jack Heuer. Thus, in 1962, the new chronographs ref. 2446 (three counters, Valjoux 72) and 3646 (two counters, Valjoux 92) appeared. These watches were the maker's first to feature an external rotating bezel and to have a name besides their references.

VERSIONS

The model was listed in the catalogue for more than 20 years, and almost 200 variants were made. There were three generations, each of which delighted famous celebrities, chiefly in the field of motor racing. The first features a 38mm case with straight lugs, Reverse Panda-type dials (see page 126) and luminous dauphine hands, which were soon replaced by baton hands (see page 22). This variant was worn by the Formula 1 driver Jochen Rindt, partner of the model Nina Lincoln (see page 84). The second introduced a new design around 1968: Jack Heuer, always in search of innovation, improved the design of the case and opted for a waterproof-type compressor patented by Piquerez (see page 148). During this period GMT complications also appeared (see page 159).

Finally, during the 1970s, the company's heyday, the new automatic calibre 11 was fitted to the watches (see page 94), which adopted a tonneau type case with the crown on the left. Jo Siffert, a driver who inspired the character played by Steve McQueen in the movie *Le Mans* (see page 94), fell in love with this model, and some say that at the time he tried to convince his associates to adopt it in the paddock. During this period, celebrities in various fields – including Bruce Springsteen and Mick Jagger – were delighted by the Autavia.

RENAISSANCE

In 1985, the Heuer group was bought by Techniques d'Avant-Garde (TAG) and the Autavia fell off the radar. In 1999, the brand was taken over by the LVMH group and, several years later, to celebrate the model's 55th anniversary, an operation was launched to resurrect it: the Autavia Cup. In the spring of 2016, enthusiasts found a website with a competition between 16 versions of the watch. The competition garnered 50,000 votes. As if symbolically, it was a first-generation 2446 that won – the same one that had belonged to Jochen Rindt. TAG Heuer therefore updated the Autavia with a new automatic movement while retaining the DNA of the original model.

MONACO

HEUER – 1969

**The first square, automatic and waterproof chronograph,
the Heuer Monaco is inextricably bound up with the actor Steve McQueen.
This watch is one of the most recognizable ever created.**

SEE OPPOSITE	1972 MODEL
MANUFACTURER	HEUER
MODEL	MONACO
REFERENCE	1533G (GREY)
DIAL	SILVER
WINDING MECHANISM	AUTOMATIC
CALIBRE	CALIBRE 15
DIAMETER	40 × 38MM
MATERIAL	STEEL
STRAP	STEEL
TYPE	GAY FRÈRES

**HEUER
CAL. 11**

In Basel on 3 March 1969, a consortium (Hamilton-Büren, Dubois Dépraz, Breitling and Heuer-Leonidas) unveiled the calibre 11, an automatic chronograph calibre designed to compete with the Zenith El Primero.

PROJET 99

At the end of the 1960s, the race to design the first automatic chronograph was on. As Zenith prepared to launch its revolutionary movement (see page 66), several manufacturers got together in the utmost secrecy to design their own and cut production costs. The consortium was named Projet 99. The automatic movement with a micro-rotor was made by Büren, based on a Dubois Dépraz chronograph module. Breitling and Heuer were in charge of financing and manufacturing the other components. All this energy led to the design of the calibre 11, known as the Chrono-Matic. It was unveiled on 3 March 1969 in Basel and fitted to various models by the different manufacturers associated with the project, despite being competitors. To accommodate this impressive movement, Jack Heuer planned to change the case of the Carrera and Autavia. At the same time, he conceived a less traditional model: the Monaco.

SQUARE, AUTOMATIC AND WATERPROOF

Two versions of the first automatic, waterproof, square chronograph were launched at the Basel trade fair, at a price of $200: a ref. 1133 B (blue) and a ref. 1133 G (grey). On its launch, the wide case (40 × 38mm) made an impact. It was the work of the manufacturer Piquerez who were specialists in the field (see page 148). Jack Heuer had just secured exclusive rights to make use of this waterproof, monocoque case, which made it possible to protect the new calibre and needed a special tool to open it (Tool 033). Another unique feature was that the crown

was on the left, for technical reasons (see page 88). In 1971, the calibre 11 was updated, and the movement was made more robust. It was now named calibre 12. However, such was the cost of manufacturing it that the following year Heuer decided to produce a simplified version, the calibre 15. With this fitted to the ref. 1533, the watch featured subsidiary seconds at 10 o'clock – in place of, and in the location of, the hour counter. That same year, some references featuring Valjoux manual movements were launched. The date at 6 o'clock was then replaced by a third subdial. The Monaco was relatively successful and the model was popularized by the TAG group, which bought the brand in 1985. From the end of the 1990s, the company did not hesitate to use Steve McQueen in its advertizing, having bought the rights to use his image.

'QUEEN OF COOL'

The Heuer Monaco was indeed inextricably bound up with Steve McQueen, thanks to the movie *Le Mans*. Jo Siffert, the Porsche team's leading driver, was a consultant during shooting. Sponsored by Heuer and equipped with an Autavia model (see page 92), Steve McQueen drew inspiration from it in playing the lead role. Highly visible throughout the film, the Monaco became one of the most recognizable watches ever created. Two watches were used in the movie. In July 2012, the first was sold at a Hollywood Memorabilia Auction for £628,700 ($799,500). The second reached dizzying heights at the auctioneers Phillips, fetching £1,736,500 ($2,208,000).

242 T

WITTNAUER – 1964

**The Wittnauer company enjoyed exclusive rights to the
Swiss brand Longines in the Unites States.
It also sold its own-brand watches.**

SEE OPPOSITE	1964 MODEL
MANUFACTURER	WITTNAUER
MODEL	PROFESSIONAL CHRONOGRAPH
REFERENCE	242 T
DIAL	BLACK
WINDING MECHANISM	MECHANICAL
CALIBRE	VALJOUX 72
DIAMETER	38MM
MATERIAL	STEEL
STRAP	LEATHER
TYPE	RALLYE

**WITTNAUER
235T**

The 235T model was one of three models
tested by NASA to equip the astronauts
on the Apollo space programme. Its
glass came loose during testing
and so it was not chosen.

AMERICAN DREAM

At the age of 16 in 1872, young Swiss
watchmaker Albert Wittnauer crossed the
Atlantic to go and work for his brother-
in-law, Eugène Robert, who ran a watch
importing business. They soon decided to
design their own models and produce them
in the United States, limiting the number
of Swiss components on which import duties
were payable. A few models were made, and
the A. Wittnauer Company, which continued
to import watches, was formed in 1890.
Eugène Robert pulled out, but Albert's two
brothers, Émile and Louis, as well as his
younger sister, Martha, joined him to offer
a helping hand. Martha took charge of the
company in 1916 and became the first woman
to run a watch manufacturing company – a
position she held for more than 20 years.
At the beginning of the 20th century,
Wittnauer specialized in tool watches.
Its first successful model was the All-Proof,
a shock-resistant, waterproof and
antimagnetic watch.

LONGINES AND WITTNAUER

The exclusive rights to sell Longines
watches in the United States had belonged
to Wittnauer since 1880, but in 1950 the
company was bought by Longines and
renamed Longines-Wittnauer Co. This
decision proved to be strategically sound, for
the two brands rapidly gained popularity
in the United States. Models that looked
identical were made, bearing different
names depending on where they were sold.
For example, the Wittnauer ref. 7004A,
featuring a Valjoux 7733, was distributed in

the American market. Its Swiss cousin, the
Longines ref. 7981, which was fitted with the
prestigious calibre 30CH, was sold on other
continents. This confusion has sometimes
led people to believe that Wittnauer was
Longines' entry-level make. Although the
two makes forged a solid bond, they
continued to produce separate watches
until the 1970s, when the quartz crisis
(see page 209) and acquisitions brought
about the US company's decline.

NON-CERTIFICATION BY NASA

In 1962, when NASA was preparing
the Apollo programme, it invited watch
manufacturers to submit bids for creating
the equipment required by the astronauts.
The engineer James H. Ragan drew up
a specification and put in place a testing
process that was to run from 21 October 1964
to 1 March 1965. The watches needed to be
readable, resistant to extreme changes in
pressure and temperature, and accurate in
measuring elapsed time. Six manufacturers
were contacted, four replied, and three
models underwent the final phases: the
Rolex Daytona, Omega Speedmaster and
Wittnauer-Longines 235T. During the tests
the first of these stopped functioning, and
the glass came off the third. The second
watch came out having been affected by the
tests but in working order, and naturally
was chosen to be NASA's official watch
(see page 98). Although it was not chosen,
Wittnauer nevertheless has a place in space
exploration history, because an All-Proof
model was used by Neil Armstrong to
complement his Speedmaster on the
Gemini VIII mission.

SPEEDMASTER

OMEGA – 1957

**In 1957, Omega launched the Speedmaster. This chronograph,
initially aimed at motor racing, took part in one of humanity's
most extraordinary adventures: the conquest of space.**

SEE OPPOSITE	1967 MODEL
MANUFACTURER	OMEGA
MODEL	SPEEDMASTER
REFERENCE	ST 145.012
DIAL	BLACK
WINDING MECHANISM	MECHANICAL
CALIBRE	321
DIAMETER	42MM
MATERIAL	STEEL
STRAP	N/A
TYPE	N/A

SPEEDMASTER

1957	CK 2915
1959	CK 2998
1962	ST 105.002
1964	ST 105.003
1964	ST 105.012
1967	ST 145.012
1968	ST 145.022

A RACING CHRONOGRAPH

Omega unveiled a trio of watches in 1957:
a dive watch, the Seamaster 300 (CK 2913)
(see page 146); an antimagnetic watch, the
Railmaster (CK 2914, see page 159); and a
racing chronograph, the Speedmaster
(CK 2915). The three models had different
uses but a common design, featuring the
broad arrow hands (see page 23) that are
also found on the Ranchero (see page 44).
The Speedmaster was designed to make its
mark on motor-racing circuits and its design,
initiated by Claude Baillod and Pierre
Moinat, was inspired by the instruments
found on Italian cars. At its launch the
Speedy, as it was named, was the first
watch with a tachymeter scale on the bezel
rather than on the dial, in order to improve
readability and, consequently, the drivers'
performance. It featured a black dial with
three counters, and was driven by the calibre
321 with a column wheel (see page 100),
which was used until 1968 (and was
produced again, in small numbers, in 2020).

THE PRE-MOON PERIOD

The Speedmaster's first journey into space
took place in 1962, on the Mercury-Atlas 8
mission on board the Sigma 7 capsule. The
astronaut Walter Schirra wore his personal
watch: a ref. CK 2998-2. This reference had
evolved since the first generation: it had
dauphine hands and the outer dial was black.
On 1 March 1965, during the development
of its space programme, NASA chose the
Speedmaster as the official chronograph after
a series of severe tests (see page 96). The
new ref. ST 105.003, now featuring baton
hands, gained certification for use in space
missions. Three months later it was used on

the Gemini IV mission by the astronaut
Ed White, when he became the first
American to walk in space.

THE FIRST WATCH ON THE MOON

Four years later, NASA's Apollo 11 space
programme was preparing to put humans
on the moon. For this exploit, the agency
acquired the latest versions of the
Speedmaster: the ST 105.012 and the
ST 145.012. In contrast to previous versions,
the word Professional appeared on the
dial and, above all, they were bulkier: the
lugs were lyre-shaped and the crown was
protected by the shape of the case, which had
increased from 39mm to 42mm. On 21 July
1969, the ST 105.012 became the first watch
worn on the moon, thanks to Buzz Aldrin,
who was the second to set foot on the moon's
surface after Armstrong, who had left his in
the module. Although it had been taken on
the mission, the ST 145.012 also remained
on board. It would be worn on the moon two
years later, during the Apollo 14 mission.
The Moonwatch figured in all subsequent
space missions. Only the movement changed,
with time and technical advances. In 1968,
the ST 145.022 replaced the calibre 321 with
the 861 with cams (without a column wheel).
That too was improved in turn with the 1861
at the end of the 1990s. Over time, numerous
limited editions were produced. Some of
these are adorned with Snoopy, a reference
to the Snoopy Award, a prestigious prize
awarded by NASA for services rendered.

OMEGA SPEEDMASTER
REF. 145.012; CALIBRE 321

Capable of withstanding shocks, changes of temperature or pressure,
acceleration and vibrations, the calibre 321 fitted to the Moonwatch
is held in especially high esteem by enthusiasts.

CALIBRE 321

FACT SHEET N°10

**A representative movement of the pre-moon
Speedmaster models, the calibre 321 was the fruit
of a collaboration between Omega and Lemania.**

ALBERT GUSTAVE PIGUET
AND THE PROJET 27 CHRO C12

Lemania was a Swiss company founded in
1884 by Alfred Lugrin that specialized in
making watch mechanisms. In 1930, Omega
merged with Tissot, then Lemania in 1932,
to create a new company: Société Suisse
pour l'Industrie Horlogère (SSIH). In 1934,
Albert Gustave Piguet was employed by
the company's technical office in L'Orient,
Switzerland. He came from a family of highly
regarded watchmakers and took the reins of
a new department working on a movement
project in collaboration with Omega: the
27 CHRO C12.

The features of the calibre appear in the
project's name: a diameter of 27mm and
a chronograph with a 12-hour counter.
Furthermore, the movement was required to
be as thin as possible with a power reserve of
46 hours. At the conclusion of the project, the
calibre was denominated 2310 by Lemania
and 321 by Omega. Featuring a column
wheel made from a single piece, a balance
oscillating at 18,000 vibrations per hour and
a distinctive triangular bridge, it was the
smallest wrist chronograph calibre with a
12-hour counter.

Made famous by the Speedmaster model,
this movement and its variants were also
used in the De Ville models, as well as by
other manufacturers such as Patek Philippe,
Vacheron and Breguet.

CALIBRE 321 AND SPEEDMASTER

The calibre 321 had its finest hour thanks
to the Speedmaster model. Used from 1957
in ref. CK 2915, it was fitted to models
until 1968 (see page 98). However, given
the success of the Speedmaster and the cost
of its manufacture, the calibre 321 with
column wheel was replaced by a new calibre,
the 861, which was simpler to produce yet
had the same high performance. However,
decades later in 2020, to everyone's surprise
and the delight of watch enthusiasts, Omega
resurrected the representative calibre 321.

ALASKA 11

For the relaunch of the calibre 321, Omega
put together a team of experts under the
code name Alaska 11 (a name already used for
other Omega projects during the 1960s and
1970s). They worked in secret for two years
to bring it back to life. Entirely manufactured
in the factory at Omega's headquarters in
Bienne, Switzerland, in a specially dedicated
workshop, each movement was assembled
by a single watchmaker. In order to remain as
faithful as possible to the original model, the
team used tomography (a digital scanner) to
look inside a Speedmaster – and not just any
Speedmaster: it was the ref. ST 105.003 that
the astronaut Eugene (Gene) Cernan wore on
the moon during the Apollo 17 mission in 1972.
The movement of the Speedmaster worn by
Cernan, the last man to walk on the moon, was
therefore the one used to faithfully reconstruct
the calibre 321.

DIALS AND MEASURING SCALES

**The dial is an essential component of a watch.
It enables the user to tell the time, but may also incorporate practical information.
Its texture, be it patterned or linked to the passage of time,
is an essential aesthetic criterion that is appreciated by enthusiasts.**

SCALES

Scales are essential for the display of certain pieces of information. The readability of minutes, and even seconds, is extremely important on certain models, especially on chronographs.

- **The minuterie**: this is the most common scale. It is also used on subdials.

- **The railway track**: when the minuterie is surrounded by lines resembling rails, connected by dashes that mark the minutes, it is also known as *chemin de fer* (railway).

- **The tachymeter**: although most tachymeters today are found on bezels, it used to be usual to place them on the dial. The tachymeter is used to measure the speed of an object (for example, a racing car). It implies the presence of a chronograph function. To use it, pick a reference point, start the chronograph, press the push-button again 1,000m (1,093yd) farther on, and look on the scale where the hand has stopped: the reading will give your average speed.

- **The pulsometer**: this scale allows the wearer to calculate someone's heart rate. Much appreciated by doctors, pulsometers are generally calibrated for 15 or 30 beats. Start the chronograph at the first heartbeat and stop it at the last (15 or 30).

You can then read the heart rate in beats per minute using the chronograph's hand.

- **The telemeter**: the telemeter scale makes it possible to measure the distance between where the watch is and another event visible to the naked eye. For example, it can be used to calculate how far away lightning struck by starting the chronometer between the flash of lightning and the sound of thunder.

TEXTURE AND DECORATION

Decoration and texture matter a great deal to collectors. They play a part in the overall aesthetic appeal of a watch.

- **Lacquering**: there are various materials and techniques for colouring and/or protecting a dial. Lacquer is the most common. During the 1950s and 1960s many watch manufacturers used a golden ink on their black lacquered dials for clear readability. A gilt dial is particularly desirable among collectors (see Rolex Oyster, page 48).

- **Dials with patterns**: these may be imprinted, using a press that imprints a motif, or engraved by a type of artisan engraving that uses a machine worked by hand. They may also be carved or set with precious stones.

- **Enamelled dials**: there are many ways to make these, including the techniques of cloisonné, champlevé and grisaille. The commonest is grand feu enamel: a special powder is applied on a rough outline of a copper dial. This is then placed in a kiln at about 800°C (1,472°F), so that the powder melts and burns on to the disc. This process is repeated until the desired thickness and colour are produced.

- **Tropical dials**: a tropical dial is that of an old watch, generally black originally down to a production error, but faded to brown over time. The more even the patina, the more desirable the watch. Patina depends on numerous factors, and the marks left by time are always different. A watch with a tropical dial is therefore unique, like a great vintage wine. The price of certain watches can double or even triple because of a uniform tropical patina.

MINUTERIE

The classic scale, found on
most watches.

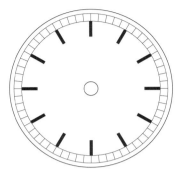

RAILWAY TRACK

A type of minuterie whose scale recalls
a railway track.

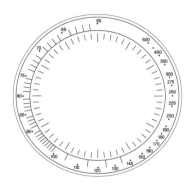

TACHYMETER

This is used to measure the speed of
an object – a racing car, for example.

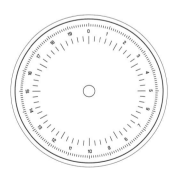

TELEMETER

This makes it possible to measure the
distance between the watch's location and
another event – for example, lightning.

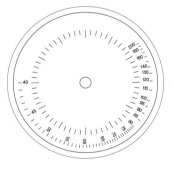

PULSOMETER

This allows the
measurement of
someone's heart rate.

AVIATION

The first watches designed for pilots appeared at the beginning of the 20th century. From the 1950s, the growing popularity of chronographs contributed to the development of professional watches dedicated to this activity.

FROM THE SANTOS-DUMONT TO THE GMT

At the beginning of the 20th century, the aviation pioneer Alberto Santos-Dumont asked Louis Cartier to create a wristwatch for him; at the time wristwatches were only worn by women (see page 32). Pocket watches were inconvenient for pilots because they were forced to let go of the controls to check the time. The result of this collaboration was the Santos-Dumont, the first men's wristwatch, but also the first watch for aeroplane pilots. In fact, it was the first watch aimed at a particular type of customer who had specific requirements. However, although today this elegant watch has become an icon, it cannot be considered to be specifically dedicated to pilots. Before the 1950s other specialized watches, which were not chronographs, appeared and were used during both world wars. This was the case with, among others, the Special Pilot's Watch created by IWC in 1936, which featured a highly readable dial, an antimagnetic movement, shatterproof glass and an oversized crown. In 1953, another non-chronograph aimed at civilian pilots was developed by Rolex: the GMT. It allowed pilots to read the local time and the time in their home country simultaneously (see page 162).

SPECIALIZED CHRONOGRAPHS

Civil and military aviation boomed during the 1950s. Breitling's expertise with chronographs encouraged this Swiss company to devote an entire department to aviation. In 1941, Breitling launched the Chronomat, the first chronograph featuring a circular logarithmic slide rule. The watch was equipped with two scales: one displayed the time, the other distance (a telemeter). This innovation allowed professionals to make all kinds of mathematical calculations. Breitling developed its own model and in 1953 launched the Co-Pilot for military users, and a year later the Navitimer (see page 106). During the same period, France's defence ministry published a technical outline for a chronograph that was to be issued to pilots: the Type 20 (see page 112). Most of the watches that matched the specification featured a flyback function, which allowed the chronograph to be zeroed at the touch of the lower button, thus simplifying operations and allowing several times to be measured consecutively. The same document demanded that dials should be readable. With time, other manufacturers developed watches aimed at pilots. The Heuer chronograph, based on one created by Leonidas, brought together all the features a pilot's chronograph required (see page 116).

CHARACTERISTICS OF A PILOT'S WATCH

There is no single type of pilot's watch, but several, and they all have common characteristics. Essentially, the watch needs to be readable and easy to operate. A pilot must be able to tell the time, whatever the weather, and when flying during the day and at night. Many watches therefore have dark dials with contrasting luminous numerals or indexes. To make them easier to operate, the first pilot's watches featured a wide crown. Similarly, the Bundeswehr (see page 116) features a large crown and easily accessible, long push-buttons, designed to be operated while wearing gloves. Whether it features a GMT bezel or a slide rule, an antimagnetic function or a flyback function, the pilot's watch is distinguished by its readability and ease of operation.

NAVITIMER

BREITLING – 1954

In 1954, Breitling created a chronograph that featured a circular slide rule for the US Aircraft Owners and Pilots Association (AOPA): the Navitimer.

SEE OPPOSITE	1967 MODEL
MANUFACTURER	BREITLING
MODEL	NAVITIMER
REFERENCEE	806
DIAL	BLACK, SMALL DIALS, ALSO BEARS THE NAME LIP
WINDING MECHANISM	MECHANICAL
CALIBRE	VENUS 178
DIAMETER	41MM
MATERIAL	STEEL
STRAP	LEATHER
TYPE	SIMPLE

DEPARTMENT EIGHT

In 1884, Léon Breitling set up a workshop specializing in counters and chronometers in Saint-Imier, Switzerland. In 1932, the company's third generation, in the form of Willy Breitling, took the reins. He registered a patent that was important in the maufacture of chronographs – a mechanism with two push-buttons that were independent of the crown: the first started and stopped the chronograph, while the second reset the hands to zero. This know-how brought Breitling into contact with specialist activities such as motor racing and, more importantly, aviation. After the launch of the first on-board chronograph in 1931, Willy Breitling devoted an entire department to them: Department Eight, the name of which was a reference to the eight-day power reserve on aviation instruments.

COLLABORATION WITH AOPA

In 1941, Breitling brought out a watch that would go on to inspire its future best seller: the Chronomat (a portmanteau word formed from 'chronograph' and 'mathematician'). It was the first chronograph to feature a circular logarithmic slide rule. It had two scales: one displayed the time, the other distance (a telemeter), so that a whole range of calculations could be made. In 1952, the US Aircraft Owners and Pilots Association (AOPA) asked Willy Breitling to create a watch for its members. The company revisited the Chronomat concept, incorporating a slide rule specially designed for aviation and to improve readability. The case was 41mm and the dial was now black, and early models had luminous Arab numerals.

It was named Navitimer (from 'navigation' and 'timer'). Neither the Breitling marque nor the reference 806 figured on the early versions, which were exclusively distributed to members of the AOPA.

PILOTS' RECEPTION

The Navitimer that was available to the wider public appeared around 1955. For the first time, the brand name appeared on its own, with no mention of AOPA, and the watch was given the reference 806. At the time most airlines were competing for long-haul routes, and the Navitimer became an essential piece of equipment for pilots. At the beginning of the 1960s, the watch was modernized with a new stylized Twin Jet logo, which showed two aeroplanes. A new kind of customer then showed an interest in this watch. It was seen at motor racing circuits but also on stage, on the wrist of the jazz musician Miles Davis. The most significant evolution of the Navitimer took place in 1969: Breitling was part of Projet 99, which aimed to develop an automatic chronograph (see page 94). In early 1970, models were fitted with the Calibre 11 Chrono-Matic, and the design changed: the crown was moved to the left and the date function added. Myriad versions then appeared, including a mechanical one, which Serge Gainsbourg acquired in 1985 and had fitted with a platinum rallye strap. This model was undoubtedly the maker's most iconic, and today remains the ultimate pilots' wristwatch.

CO-PILOT

BREITLING – 1953

**In 1953, while the Navitimer was still being developed,
Breitling's Department Eight, which specialized in aviation,
launched its first creation: the Co-Pilot.**

SEE OPPOSITE	**1966 MODEL**
MANUFACTURER	**BREITLING**
MODEL	**CO-PILOT**
REFERENCE	**765 AVI**
DIAL	**BLACK, REVERSE PANDA, ALSO BEARS THE NAME LIP**
WINDING MECHANISM	**MECHANICAL**
CALIBRE	**VENUS 178**
DIAMETER	**41MM**
MATERIAL	**STEEL**
STRAP	**LEATHER**
TYPE	**SIMPLE**

VENUS
CAL. 178

Chronograph movements with a
column wheel are the most prestigious.
The Venus 178, used by Breitling,
is especially celebrated for its
structure and refinement.

MILITARY CHRONOGRAPH

In 1953, while the AOPA Navitimer was still under development, Breitling's Department Eight (see page 106) launched its first creation: the Co-Pilot (ref. 765 AVI). While the Navitimer was aimed at civil aviation pilots, the Co-Pilot's calling was essentially military. As a result, this model's functions were simpler when compared to those of its younger sibling, to meet the needs of soldiers, whatever the situation they found themselves in. Consequently, the emphasis was on robustness and readability. The watch did not feature a slide rule. It had a rotating bezel engraved from 1 to 12 that offered both a second chronograph function and a second time zone. The subdials on the dial were initially completely black. At the beginning of the 1960s, as with the Navitimer, they became white and silver (Reverse Panda, see page 126). Alongside its military use, the aptly named Co-Pilot was intended to complement the Navitimer for pilots in the Breitling catalogue.

RAQUEL WELCH

In the mid-1960s the Reverse Panda version of this watch was the height of modern style. Its pared-down, readable design was popular, and in France this watch was often found bearing a second name – LIP – which at the time was the world's sixth-biggest watchmaker (see page 56). The watch delighted sports personalities such as the famous racing driver Ken Miles and the skier Jean-Claude Killy. But it was the American actor, Raquel Welch, who popularized the model – it is named after her by collectors today. The story that links the watch and

the actor dates from 1967, at a time when the star was playing a parachutist in the movie *Fathom*. The plot involves an espionage agency hiring Fathom Harvill, played by Welch, to infiltrate the enemy and retrieve the trigger for an atomic bomb. To lend credibility to the character, the prop masters naturally opted for a Breitling ref. 765 AVI, the model having already proved itself in the French and Italian armies.

CONTEMPORARY DESIGN

Such was its success that several versions of this chronograph appeared at the end of the 1960s. Breitling offered the Co-Pilot Unitime (ref. 1765), which made it possible to tell the time in two time zones thanks to its 24-hour dial and rotating bezel. Another version, the Co-Pilot Yachting (ref. 7650), was intended for navigation, and made it possible to measure the countdown to the start of a regatta (see page 121). At the beginning of the 1970s, automatic versions, fitted with the Chrono-Matic calibre and developed in partnership with Heuer-Leonidas and Büren-Hamilton (see page 94), appeared. Over time the design changed, and numerous variants were launched. However, in 2020 Breitling paid homage to its cult model: the brand created an almost-exact reproduction of a 1953 model, much to the delight of enthusiasts – proof that the design was perfect from the start.

AIR COMMAND

BLANCPAIN – 1960

**The Air Command was a watch aimed at pilots.
Produced in small numbers, it is often considered the most desirable
military chronograph of the 1950s and 1960s.**

SEE OPPOSITE	**1960 MODEL**
MANUFACTURER	**BLANCPAIN**
MODEL	**AIR COMMAND**
REFERENCE	**1735**
DIAL	**BLACK**
WINDING MECHANISM	**MECHANICAL**
CALIBRE	**VALJOUX 222**
DIAMETER	**42MM**
MATERIAL	**STEEL**
STRAP	**LEATHER**
TYPE	**RALLYE**

VALJOUX
CAL. 222

The Valjoux 222 is a modified Valjoux
22 with flyback function. It was made
for 60 years and used in some Airain
Type 20 watches supplied to the
French Air Force.

MYSTERIOUS ORIGIN

Blancpain is one of the world's oldest
watchmakers. Founded in 1735, over the
decades it established itself in the world of
watchmaking and never succumbed to quartz
movements. In 1953, the company developed
the first military dive watch: the Fifty
Fathoms (see page 132). The history of the
Air Command pilot's chronograph is less well
documented and more mysterious: its origin
is supposedly bound up with that of the
Type 20 watches and the American market.
During the 1950s, the French defence and
armed forces ministry decided to supply its
pilots with reliable instruments that included
a flyback function (see below) and published
a specification sheet, named Type 20. At the
end of the decade, the Americans, to whom
Blancpain had successfully sold the Fifty
Fathoms to be used by their navy, went in
search of an instrument similar to the Type 20
for the US Air Force. Blancpain then designed
a chronograph that was inspired by it, and
offered it to American military pilots through
the retailer Allen V. Tornek.

A PILOT'S WATCH

Although there are several types of pilot's
watch (see page 105), many chronographs
designed for aviation have distinctive
features that are also found in the Blancpain
Air Command. Its suitability is therefore
beyond doubt, and the legend of its origin is
plausible. The watch has a large diameter
(42mm), a bi-directional countdown bezel
that is useful for pilots and is especially
readable. Both its dial, which features Arabic
numerals embellished with a tachymeter, and
its hands, are luminous. Most importantly,
the watch is driven by a Valjoux 222 flyback

movement. This function, invented by
Longines, allows the chronograph function
to be reset to zero simply by pressing the
lower push-button, thus simplifying the
pilot's tasks and making it possible to
measure several consecutive periods of time.
Watches have always accompanied pilots
on their aerial exploits and, to help them in
their missions, watchmakers have invented
various functions; of these flyback is probably
the most useful.

THE RAREST MILITARY
CHRONOGRAPH

The Air Command legend was fuelled by the
fact that Blancpain supposedly produced
only a dozen prototypes. Although the
manufacturer offered these watches to the
US Air Force, no order appears to have
been placed. The project for this model thus
remained at the study stage. Moreover, of
the few watches known to exist, some have
Blancpain movements, others do not. Many
see this as a sign that they were sold off as
spare parts and assembled belatedly. Be
that as it may, it is precisely this limited
production run and element of mystery that
make this watch so desirable. Its reputation
has made it the most sought-after military
chronograph of the late 1950s and early
1960s. To make watch enthusiasts happy,
the company faithfully recreated the model
in 2020, producing 500 examples.

TYPE 20

AURICOSTE – 1954

**Among pilots' watches, one name resonates more than the rest: the Type 20.
This type of chronograph, designed by several manufacturers, was a response
to a specification sheet published by the French defence ministry in 1953.**

1. SEE OPPOSITE

MANUFACTURER	AURICOSTE
MODEL	TYPE 20 1955
REFERENCE	N/A
DIAL	TROPICAL
WINDING MECHANISM	MECHANICAL
CALIBRE	LEMANIA CAL. 2040
DIAMETER	38MM
MATERIAL	STEEL
STRAP	LEATHER
TYPE	RALLYE

2. SEE OVERLEAF, LEFT

MANUFACTURER	VIXA
MODEL	TYPE 20 1955
REFERENCE	N/A
DIAL	BLACK
WINDING MECHANISM	MECHANICAL
CALIBRE	HANHART 4054
DIAMETER	38MM
MATERIAL	STEEL
STRAP	LEATHER
TYPE	RALLYE

3. SEE OVERLEAF, RIGHT

MANUFACTURER	BREGUET
MODEL	TYPE XX 1960
REFERENCE	N/A
DIAL	BLACK
WINDING MECHANISM	MECHANICAL
CALIBRE	VALJOUX 225
DIAMETER	38MM
MATERIAL	STEEL
STRAP	LEATHER
TYPE	SIMPLE

ORIGIN OF TYPE 20 WATCHES

The history of these watches begins in 1953,
when the French defence ministry published
a technical outline for a chronograph to
be used to equip pilots: the Type 20. This
specification sheet was inspired by the
watches used by the Luftwaffe (German air
force) during World War II, especially the
Hanhart and Tutima models. An invitation
to tender was issued, to which several watch
manufacturers responded. Four were chosen:
Breguet, Vixa (which was largely inspired
by the Hanhart), Auricoste and Dodane
(under the designations Dodane, Airain and
Chronofixe). The watches, chiefly supplied
to the French Air Force from 1954, and
subsequently to the flight testing centre and
the naval air force, were supplied to pilots
as part of their equipment. They were the
property of the French state, which was
responsible for their maintenance until they
were taken out of service.

SPECIFICATION SHEET

The specification sheet drawn up by
the French ministry allowed the watch
manufacturers a certain freedom of
interpretation. However, some of the criteria
were recommended, though not compulsory:

- a black dial with two or three counters
  (able to time a minimum of 30 minutes);
- luminous hands and Arabic numerals;
- a diameter close to 38mm;
- a bi-directional bezel;
- accuracy that deviated by no more than
  8 seconds per day;
- a power reserve greater than 35 hours;
- able to withstand 300 cycles of starting the
  chronograph (start/stop/reset to zero);

- a flyback function (see page 105): the
  chronograph is reset to zero simply by
  pressing the lower push-button. This
  makes it possible to measure several
  periods of time consecutively.

According to this outline, chronographs are
meant to undergo a full service every year.
Today most of the models encountered have
'FG XX/XX/XXXX' engraved on the caseback,
for the simple reason that at each service
the guarantee expiry date was marked on
the back. It is thus possible for collectors to
retrace the story of their watch.

TYPE 21

The freedom of interpretation of the
first specification sheet was tightened in
1956 with the Type 21, which was more
restrictive. Specifically, it made the flyback
function a requirement. It should be noted,
however, that this did not replace the Type
20, with which it coexisted for years. Given
the success of these models, and as a result
of strong demand, Breguet also produced
a civilian version, which could be bought
by private pilots or simply by lovers of fine
watches. According to archive records, these
models are denominated Type XX, not
Type 20 like the military models.

BUNDESWEHR

HEUER – 1967

In 1967, Heuer received an order from the Bundeswehr, the armed forces of the Federal Republic of Germany, for watches to be used to equip its air force.

SEE OPPOSITE	1970 MODEL
MANUFACTURER	HEUER
MODEL	BUNDESWEHR
REFERENCE	1550 SG
DIAL	BLACK
WINDING MECHANISM	MECHANICAL
CALIBRE	VALJOUX 230
DIAMETER	42MM
MATERIAL	STEEL
STRAP	N/A
TYPE	N/A

**LEONIDAS
CP2**

The Bundeswehr was a
development of the CP2 model
made by Leonidas, which was
bought by Heuer in 1964.

1964 – ACQUISITION OF LEONIDAS

The story of the watch manufacturer Leonidas began in 1841, in Saint-Imier, Switzerland. Its founder, Julien Bourquin, essentially made fob watches, but was deeply interested in the measurement of short periods of time. The Leonidas brand, which was reserved for precision watches, appeared in 1903. When it was sold two years later it took the name Leonidas Watch Factory. The years following the end of World War II were its heyday and numerous chronographs fitted with Venus or Valjoux movements were made (see page 79). During the 1960s, Leonidas felt the effects of competition from Heuer, but the company distinguished itself one last time, supplying the Italian air force with splendid flyback chronographs (see page 105): the Tipo CP1 and CP2 (*cronometro da polso*). However, on 1 January 1964, despite attempts at diversification, the company merged with its rival Heuer.

1967 – ORDER FROM THE BUNDESWEHR

In 1967, Heuer received an order from the Bundeswehr, the armed forces of the Federal Republic of Germany, which were then in the throes of a reorganization. The aim was to furnish the Luftwaffe – the air force – with the best equipment. It had just taken delivery of some C-160 aircraft, Transall's first transport aeroplanes, and wanted the best chronographs on the market for its pilots. Heuer used the model by Leonidas, the company it had just acquired, as its base – specifically the 42mm size (the first was 38mm) – to design the reference 1550 SG. The shape of the case was modified to make it less angular – but the watch's features

were unchanged. Originally designed for German pilots, it was also chosen by their Norwegian and Yugoslav counterparts. Its versatility also appealed to ground forces.

VARIANTS

Readability and functionality were the operative words with this archetypal pilot's chronograph. Its diameter (42mm) and thickness (12mm) were substantial, the bi-directional bezel was covered with a very tough PVD (physical vapour deposition) coating, the push-buttons were long, to make them easy to find in flight, the case was sandblasted to prevent any reflections and the luminous hands all looked clearly different (the arrow-shaped end of the chronograph hand stood out). The watch's construction was special too: in order to make servicing quicker, the caseback was held in place by four screws that also secured the glass. Several Valjoux movements – all of them flyback – were fitted to this chronograph during its lifespan: 22, 220 and 230. As on the Type 20 (see page 112), the dial had Arabic numerals to make it easier to read. Collectors have identified more than 20 variants. As well as the name Heuer, some display a circle containing the letters '3 H', a reference to tritium, a luminous material with an atomic mass equal to three.

FLIGHTMASTER

OMEGA – 1969

A true Swiss Army knife of a watch, the Flightmaster first appeared in the Omega catalogue in 1969. It equipped the Soviet astronauts on the Apollo-Soyuz space programme in 1975.

SEE OPPOSITE	1973 MODEL
MANUFACTURER	OMEGA
MODEL	FLIGHTMASTER
REFERENCE	ST 145.036
DIAL	SLATE GREY, COLOURED HANDS
WINDING MECHANISM	MECHANICAL
CALIBRE	911
DIAMETER	43MM
MATERIAL	STEEL
STRAP	STEEL
TYPE	1162

OMEGA
FLIGHTMASTER
HANDS

Although the dials are made in many different colours, all Flightmaster models feature a blue hour hand shaped like an aeroplane.

MASTERY OF THE SKIES

The first mention of the name Flightmaster predates the launch of the trio of watches named Railmaster, Seamaster and Speedmaster (see page 98). The manufacturer's early interest in aeronautics is demonstrated by the fact that the name was registered on 9 July 1957. In 1959, it was used for a special version of the Railmaster (an antimagnetic model made by Omega), produced for the Peruvian Air Force, which wanted a name that was more evocative of its work. It was only in around 1968, when Omega developed a professional watch for civilian and military pilots, that the name was officially applied to a model. At a time when air travel was booming, it had a specific design and functions, and was also aimed at intercontinental travellers.

CAS 22

The Flightmaster is acknowledged to be a true Swiss Army knife of a watch. Frédéric Robert, creator of the Aquastar dive watches (see page 152), approached the Lemania company (see page 100) requesting a design for the ultimate professional watch. He was appointed as a consultant, and, with Omega, took part in the development of project Cas 22. In 1969, the Flightmaster finally appeared in the catalogue. It featured a case named Pilot Line, that fitted the shape of the wrist, was waterproof to a depth of 60m for the early generations and 120m for the last, and had been developed in partnership with Piquerez (see page 148). There were numerous variations of the dial and hands, but all were contrasting so that they complied with the main criterion for a pilot's watch: readability.

It sported a large number of elements: seven hands, three crowns, two push-buttons and one internal bezel. The idea was to offer three functions: a second time zone (GMT function, see page 159) with the blue hand, a complete chronograph for calculating time intervals and a partial chronograph, thanks to the rotating bezel, that allowed flight duration to be measured without needing to start the normal chronograph function.

THE APOLLO-SOYUZ PROGRAMME

While NASA supplied its astronauts with equipment that had been officially tested for its missions (see page 96), Soviet cosmonauts were equipped with a variety of watches made in Russia. At the beginning of the 1970s, an exception was made with the general use of Omega chronographs. According to the Omega specialists Anthony Marquié and Grégoire Rossier, this choice was due to several reasons. First of all, American astronauts wore their Omega chronographs when being photographed by the press. Second, the Kremlin, which before the 1980s was more politically open, had reportedly agreed to turn to the West to equip its astronauts. The story goes that an Omega sales representative supposedly said to the Soviet cosmonauts: 'If you want to keep in time with the Americans, you ought to wear the same watch.'

MULTIFUNCTION

CHRONOGRAPHS

> During the 1960s, as chronographs flooded the market,
> some manufacturers offered models designed for navigation
> as well as multifunction watches.

REGATTA CHRONOGRAPHS

The link between watchmaking and the sea goes back to the 18th century, with navy chronographs. Concerned about their survival on expeditions to distant regions, naval officers bought large format watches designed to keep time on board ship from the best watchmakers, such as Berthoud. This relationship continued during the 1960s as a result of the democratization of nautical sports, especially regattas. At the start of a race, it is essential to manoeuvre the boat into the best possible position to gain maximum advantage. Since the race start is preceded by a five-minute countdown, the function of a regatta watch is to display the time remaining before the starting gun, from the moment the countdown has begun.

The concept was formulated in 1961, when JeanRichard (see page 152) registered a patent for a model featuring a five-minute countdown function consisting of discs. Frédéric Robert, who took over the brand and named it Aquastar, developed the Aquastar Régate. Various approaches to the function were tried during the 1960s. The first concerned standard chronographs: the minute timers were simply adapted to nautical use (see page 122). Another consisted of adding a calibrated rotating internal or external bezel to the watch, which enabled the countdown to be displayed. Some special series of the Breitling Co-Pilot model combined these two approaches (see page 108).

The most iconic regatta watch is unquestionably the Yachtingraf, of which there were several versions featuring two or three counters, as well as a model whose counter jumped every 30 seconds before the start (see page 122). Much later, Rolex launched its Yacht-Master model. In 2007, the more advanced Yacht-Master II became the world's first watch with a mechanical memory to feature a countdown that was programmable from one to 10 minutes.

MULTIPLE FUNCTIONS

A period of reconstruction and innovation followed World War II. Humanity strove to conquer new horizons: the depths of the sea, the highest points of the globe, the sky and space. Watchmaking developed new ideas in parallel with this. During the 1950s and 1960s, Swiss manufacturers created watches with evermore specific applications. Their attention focused on two main areas: dive watches and chronographs. The biggest manufacturers (Rolex, Heuer, Omega, Breitling, etc.) developed historic lines that are still sold today. In 1963 the *Journal Suisse d'Horlogerie* published an insert showing nine chronographs, including a Nivada (see page 126), accompanied by the words: 'Your son does not respect your watch in the slightest. He is of an age that runs on chronograph time.' Young people were the new target market: their activities included motor racing, skiing, athletics and sailing.

It was in this context that the Chronomaster appeared. It combined a chronograph function with waterproofing to a depth of 200m, a tachymeter bezel, a rotating dive bezel, a second time zone on the bezel and a regatta timer. At the time it was the only watch to combine so many functions.

YACHTINGRAF

YEMA – 1967

In 1966, Yema registered two patents for a watch aimed specifically at the world of sailing. And Yachtingraf, the famous chronograph with the tricolour counter, was born.

MANUFACTURER	YEMA

1. SEE OPPOSITE

MODEL	YACHTINGRAF RÉGATE BLUE SHIP 1970
REFERENCE	5667370
DIAL	BLACK
WINDING MECHANISM	MECHANICAL
CALIBRE	7733 SPECIAL
DIAMETER	41MM
MATERIAL	STEEL
STRAP	LEATHER
TYPE	RALLYE

2. SEE OVERLEAF, LEFT

MODEL	YACHTINGRAF CROISIÈRE 1969
REFERENCE	93012
DIAL	BLACK
WINDING MECHANISM	MECHANICAL
CALIBRE	7736
DIAMETER	38MM
MATERIAL	STEEL
STRAP	LEATHER
TYPE	SIMPLE

YEMA – A FRENCH STORY

The story of this young manufacturer, founded in Besançon by Henry-Louis Belmont, begins in 1948. From the 1950s, the company distinguished itself by creating shock-resistant watches, followed by the first waterproof watches (with a Skin Diver series) and chronographs. Although certain components were French-made, like its peers at the time the brand used *ébauches* for its movements. The company was soon successful, both in France and internationally. In 1960, it was the biggest French exporter, producing 220,000 watches. During that decade, it acquired a 20-atm (200-m) water-resistance tester, for watches designed for use at great depths. In around 1967, the first mass-produced French watch that was waterproof to a depth of 300m appeared: the Superman.

YACHTINGRAF

In 1966, Yema registered two patents for a chronograph aimed specifically at the world of sailing, described in the patent for the United States as 'Watch for yachting and underwater use' and as the 'Chronoscope' in that for Switzerland. And so the Yachtingraf and its tricolour counter appeared. Its function was simple. At a regatta, the aim is to position the boat to gain an advantage at the start of the race. This is preceded by a five-minute countdown. Thanks to its counter, the watch made it possible to see exactly how much time remained. However, this patent applied only to an ingenious way of using the counter; there was no change to the movement. At least seven versions of this watch exist with different types of case or movement. Although the version with two counters is highly sought after, the version of the Yachtingraf Croisière with three counters is even more desirable. The latter features a Valjoux 7736 with cams if its second counter is black, and a Valjoux 72 with column wheel if the counter is white. The Régate variant, fitted with a Valjoux 7733 S (Spécial), appeared in around 1970. In contrast to the usual configuration, the counter jumps every 30 seconds before the start, in order to increase its accuracy.

A PASSPORT TO PARTNERSHIPS

The reliability and robustness of its watches earned Yema a solid reputation, and allowed it to partner with several organizations. The Superman, waterproof to a depth of 300m, was used by rescue divers from the French Air Force. The Yachtingraf was chosen by the French sailing federation. Éric Tabarly, who was often associated with the LIP Nautic-Ski, was delighted by this waterproof chronograph. Another, the Rallygraf, was appreciated by racing drivers, including Mario Andretti. During the 1980s, Yema formed a partnership with the Centre National d'Etudes Spatiales (CNES) (French National Space Studies Centre), and several versions of the Spationaute model were worn on space flights by Jean-Loup Chrétien and Patrick Baudry. At the same time, the North Pole model was used by Jean-Louis Étienne on his 800-km (500-mile) solo walk towards the North Pole.

CHRONOMASTER

NIVADA - 1961

**In the mid-1960s, the Chronomaster Aviator Sea Diver model appeared.
In the United States, this super-chronograph, designed by Nivada,
was sold under the name Croton.**

MANUFACTURER	NIVADA

1. SEE OPPOSITE

MODEL	CASD BIG EYE DE 1965
REFERENCE	85006
DIAL	BLACK
WINDING MECHANISM	MECHANICAL
CALIBRE	VALJOUX 23
DIAMETER	38MM
MATERIAL	STEEL
STRAP	N/A
TYPE	N/A

2. SEE PREVIOUS PAGE, RIGHT

MODEL	CASD PANDA 1965
REFERENCE	105/9839
DIAL	WHITE PANDA
WINDING MECHANISM	MECHANICAL
CALIBRE	VALJOUX 92
DIAMETER	38MM
MATERIAL	STEEL
STRAP	LEATHER
TYPE	RALLYE

PANDA DIAL

During the 1960s watches for racing drivers appeared and their readability was crucial. Models such as the Autavia (see page 92) and the Daytona (see page 72) featured contrasting subdials, generally black with white counters or white with black counters. White models with black counters, which were rarer, were dubbed Panda by collectors. The others were nicknamed Reverse Panda.

SPECIALIZATION OF TOOL WATCHES

Nivada has been active in the watchmaking industry since 1926, when Jacob Schneider formed the company in Granges (Grenchen), Switzerland. In the United States, the Croton company, which had been in existence since 1878, distributed its watches. Consequently, it is possible to find watches bearing the name Nivada, Croton or both. The designation, which differed according to the country in which the watches were sold, was the result of (unsuccessful) legal proceedings brought by Movado, which claimed the name Nivada was too close to its own. From the 1950s onwards, several models of tool watch (which had a function other than telling the time) were launched. The first successful one was undoubtedly the waterproof, automatic Antarctic model, which was used by members of the Deep Freeze polar expedition. During the 1960s, Nivada distinguished itself in the dive watch sector with the Depthomatic, the first watch to feature a depth gauge, and then with the Depthmaster which could withstand a pressure of 100atm (1,000m). The Chronomaster appeared during this period. Depending on the country where it was sold, this model can be found under five different names: Nivada, Nivada Grenchen, Croton, Croton Nivada Grenchen and Croton 1878.

'SUPER-CHRONOGRAPH'

The Chronomaster was not a simple chronograph but rather, as brochures from the time state, a 'super-chronograph'. The intention was indeed perfectly conveyed in the model's full name: Chronomaster Aviator Sea Diver. This denomination implied multiple functions and was aimed at a broad market: racing drivers, pilots, sailors and even divers. Compared to what other manufacturers offered at the time, it is striking that the Chronomaster combines a multitude of interesting features: a chronograph function, waterproofing to 200m, a tachymeter bezel, a rotating dive bezel, a second time zone on the bezel and a regatta timer. Despite these features being common to all models, a multitude of variants, with different colours, brand names, marks and typefaces were released. They were fitted with quality movements, initially made by Venus, then by Valjoux (see page 79) or Landeron. The first appearance of the model dates from 1961, in a catalogue distributed in the United States, a country where the Chronomaster sold widely. At that time, technological developments were speeding up and humanity was discovering new horizons. In parallel with this, watchmakers were creating evermore professional watches. Nivada flaunted itself alongside the greats, such as Heuer, Breitling, Omega and Rolex, even though its production lasted only a decade. Following the quartz crisis of the 1970s (see page 209), Nivada and Croton were forced to relinquish their activities. After being bought and sold several times, the brand was reborn in 2020 and now offers models identical to the finest ones made during the 1960s.

DIVE
WATCHES

CHAPTER 3

BLANCPAIN FIFTY FATHOMS
'SUBASE 4' CASEBACK

The origin of Subase watches is mysterious and only a few examples are known.
They have the same engraving as, and are individually numbered like, the Fifty Fathoms
and Tudor Submariner (ref. 7928) models delivered to US Navy bases.

DIVE WATCHES

To qualify as a dive watch, a model must be able to withstand great depths, feature a rotating bezel indicating the length of the dive and be visible in the dark.

WATERPROOFING

In 1883, in Saint-Imier, Switzerland, a watchmaking company named Alcide Droz & Fils had the idea of fitting a waterproof seal to the winding crown of one of its fob watches. The first waterproof watch – prudently named L'Imperméable ('The Raincoat' or 'The Waterproof One') – was born. Hot on its heels, the boom in wristwatches led manufacturers to mass-produce waterproof watches. In 1926, Rolex unveiled the Oyster, its first sports watch (see page 48). To demonstrate that it was waterproof, the manufacturer gave one to the swimmer Mercedes Gleitze to wear on her crossing of the English Channel. Then came Omega's Marine, which could withstand the pressure at a depth of 135m, followed by Mido's Multifort Aquadura, the first automatic and shock-resistant waterproof watch, and finally, in 1948, the rugged Seamaster watches (see page 58).

THE DEVELOPMENT OF DIVE WATCHES

The world of diving was revolutionized after World War II thanks to the invention of the diving mechanism and the perfection of diving cylinders containing compressed air, which made much longer dives possible. In 1952, the French defence ministry gave Robert Maloubier the task of setting up an elite unit of combat swimmers. He turned to Blancpain to design the watch that would

equip them (see page 132). The result – named Fifty Fathoms – could withstand the pressure at a depth of 50 fathoms (91.45m). Immediately afterwards, Rolex unveiled its first Submariner, which was waterproof to 100m and was also sold by Tudor (see pages 134 and 140). At the same time, Zodiac launched its Seawolf model and Piquerez SA registered patents for a revolutionary case it had invented: the deeper the watch was submerged, the more pressure was exerted on the caseback, and the more the toric seal was compressed. Numerous manufacturers used these cases. In 1957, Omega launched the Seamaster 300, which was able to withstand immersion to a depth of 200m. It became the watch of choice for famous explorers, including Jacques-Yves Cousteau's crew on the Précontinent II expedition (see page 146). More innovations followed. In 1958, JeanRichard registered a patent for a rotating bezel, and his successor Frédéric Robert founded Aquastar (see page 152). Thanks to its toric joints, the 500 could withstand the pressure at a depth of 500m. Two chronographs, the Airstar and the Deepstar, followed. At the same time, Nivada launched the Depthomatic, the first watch to feature a depth gauge, followed by the Depthmaster, which was capable of withstanding pressures down to a depth of 1,000m, as well as a line of multifunction chronographs (see page 126). In 1967, the Doxa concept watch, which could be recognized by its orange dial, was

the first 100 per cent professional dive watch to be available to the wider public. Soon afterwards it featured an innovation: a helium release valve (see page 154). In 1972, after years of research and collaboration with Comex, Omega launched the Ploprof, an exceptional watch whose monocoque case featured a system of overcompressed joints that offered exceptional performance (see page 144). The Seamaster 1000 – which until 2009 was the world's most waterproof watch – followed, as did many others.

SPECIAL FEATURES

To be classed as a dive watch, a watch must meet three criteria. First, it must be able to withstand a deep dive. Although today there exist a multitude of designs, at the time a screwed caseback and screw-down crown were preferred. The watch must also feature a secure system for measuring the length of the dive: this is the rotating bezel, which makes it possible to calculate diving sessions. Finally, the measuring system must be perfectly visible – so the bezel (like the dial and hands) is luminous.

Today these three criteria are complemented by the ISO standard 6425. This states that dive watches must be able to withstand the pressure to a depth of at least 100m.

FIFTY FATHOMS

BLANCPAIN – 1953

Featuring a readable dial and a unidirectional bezel, the Fifty Fathoms was developed
at the request of officers in the French navy and was manufactured for military use.
It set a standard for professional dive watches.

SEE OPPOSITE	1955 MODEL
MANUFACTURER	BLANCPAIN
MODEL	FIFTY FATHOMS
REFERENCE	N/A
DIAL	BLACK
WINDING MECHANISM	AUTOMATIC
CALIBRE	1361
DIAMETER	41MM
MATERIAL	STEEL
STRAP	LEATHER
TYPE	SIMPLE

BLANCPAIN
ROTATING BEZEL

Of the three patents registered by
Blancpain, one relates to a unidirectional
bezel with a locking system, creating a
safer means of tracking a dive time.

THE FIRST DIVE WATCH

The Fifty Fathoms was created at the start
of the 1950s and was the result of a meeting
between three men: the Swiss CEO of
Blancpain Jean-Jacques Fiechter, Captain
Robert Maloubier and Lieutenant Claude
Riffaud, who had been tasked with setting
up an elite unit of combat swimmers by the
French defence ministry. In order to equip
the swimmers, the government department
initially tested watches chosen by a
Parisian wholesaler. They proved to be too
small, difficult to read and not sufficiently
waterproof. It then decided to create its
own measuring instrument by turning to
Fiechter, who was himself a keen diver.

INNOVATIVE DESIGN

The two officers, for whom this watch was
an essential part of a divers' equipment,
drew up a list of criteria it must meet.
The watch must have a black dial; large
numerals; clear indications in the form of
triangles, circles and squares; as well as
an exterior, pivoting bezel. Above all, they
wanted their swimmers to be able to align
the bezel in relation to the large minute
hand, so that the remaining time of the
dive was displayed. Jean-Jacques Fiechter
was not short of ideas for the watch. He
registered three patents: a double-locked
crown system, a caseback screwed with toric
joints and a unidirectional bezel fitted with a
locking system. He envisaged it would have
a greater diameter than other watches at
the time (41mm), feature luminous hands
and indexes and be protected from magnetic
fields. Finally, to minimize wear to the crown
he fitted it with an automatic movement.

Capable of resisting the pressure at a depth
of 91.45m the model, developed in 1952, was
named Fifty Fathoms. It was unveiled a year
later in Basel, and set the standard for dive
watches for years to come.

VARIANTS

Initially designed for use by the armed forces,
the watch was a resounding success among
diving enthusiasts thanks to the 1956 movie
Le Monde du Silence (*The Silent World*),
which featured the crew of the *Calypso*
wearing Fifty Fathoms watches. Numerous
variants then appeared, and the watch can
be found under different brand names: the
first versions, sold by Spirotechnique, a
company linked to Captain Cousteau, were
named Aqualung. This watch also equipped
other armed forces, notably the US Navy.
Owing to the restrictions that allowed only
companies established in the United States
to supply them, the watches were sold
through a distributor, Allen Tornek, and
were given the name Tornek-Rayville, with
the descriptor Milspec 1. Later, a moisture
indicator was added: a circle that changed
colour at the slightest water penetration.
During the 1960s, 'no radiation' versions
appeared, to draw attention to the use of
tritium, which is not radioactive, in place of
radium. The Fifty Fathoms is still a flagship
watch in the Blancpain range today.

SUBMARINER

ROLEX - 1953

**The first dive watch aimed at the wider public,
the Rolex Submariner has been associated with legendary
adventures in the depths of the ocean since 1953.**

MANUFACTURER	ROLEX

1. SEE OPPOSITE

MODEL	SUBMARINER 1972
REFERENCE	1680
DIAL	BLACK, RED LETTERING
WINDING MECHANISM	AUTOMATIC
CALIBRE	1575
DIAMETER	40MM
MATERIAL	STEEL
STRAP	STEEL
TYPE	OYSTER

2. SEE OVERLEAF

MODEL	SUBMARINER 1957
REFERENCE	6536
DIAL	BLACK, 4 LINE OCC
WINDING MECHANISM	AUTOMATIC
CALIBRE	1030
DIAMETER	38MM
MATERIAL	STEEL
STRAP	STEEL
TYPE	OYSTER

THE CONQUEST OF THE DEEP

In 1953, Rolex designed a prototype watch to accompany Auguste and Jacques Piccard on a dive to the bottom of the sea: the Deep Sea Special no. 1. For this dive Auguste used a vehicle he had just designed, the bathyscaphe *Trieste*. The watch was attached to the hull of the vessel, which reached a depth of 3,150m in the Mediterranean Sea. When it reappeared at an auction held by Christie's in 2020, it was still in working order and sold for almost £1.7 million (€2 million). Until 1960, a total of seven such watches were made by Rolex. Prototype no. 3 withstood a descent to 10,916m in the Mariana Trench during a second expedition undertaken by Jacques Piccard and Don Walsh. It was exhibited at the Smithsonian Museum in Washington. About 30 Deep Sea Specials were sold besides the seven prototypes, but thanks to Wilsdorf, the founder of Rolex, it was another creation that benefited from the publicity generated by these exploits: the Submariner.

1954 – COMMERCIAL PRODUCTION

Designed in 1953, at the same time as the Explorer (see page 54), the Submariner was unveiled a year later in Basel. The first generations, 38mm in size, did not yet feature a crown guard. The refs. 6204 and 6205 were known as Small Crown – the crown was 6mm – and were waterproof to 100m. Initially this model had baton hands; later it was given Mercedes hands (see page 22). In 1955, the ref. 6200 (Big Crown – 8mm) had a thicker case and was waterproof to 200m. The Submariner was improved thanks to the ref. 6536 Small Crown, which was waterproof to 100m, and ref. 6538 Big Crown, which was

waterproof to 200m and featured the 1030 calibre. The Submariner grew in popularity thanks to James Bond and his adventures with Dr No. The last generations without a crown guard appeared in around 1958, and bore the ref. 5510 and 5508.

PERPETUAL EVOLUTION

The introduction of the ref. 5512 in 1959 marked the point where the Submariner began to resemble the watch we know today. The shape changed several times and the case was enlarged to 40mm. The 6mm and 8mm crowns were replaced by a new 7mm one protected by a crown guard. The watch had a non-chronometer calibre, the 1530, which was later replaced by the 1560/70 certified chronometers, and was manufactured until 1982. In parallel, from 1962 Rolex offered the ref. 5513, driven by the 1530 movement, which was later replaced by the 1520. Both were non-chronometers. In 1969, the first Submariner featuring a date aperture and Cyclops glass was launched: the ref. 1680. Featuring a calibre 1575, it bore the word Submariner in red on the dial until 1975. It was made of steel and a gold variant was available – the tool watch had become a luxury watch. Rolex continued to develop its classic: the ref. 16800 featured sapphire glass, was waterproof down to 300m and had a unidirectional bezel. In 2003, the bezel of ref. 16610 was coloured green to mark the model's 50th anniversary. Modern Submariners remain faithful to previous models, despite the diameter being increased to 41mm and new materials being used in their manufacture.

THE ROLEX OYSTER PERPETUAL

SUBMARINER 100

For deep-sea diving and all sea-going activities

**Special Oyster case guaranteed waterproof to <u>330 ft</u>!
New "Time Recorder" rim; acts as stop watch for
timing dives
Selfwound by rotor Perpetual mechanism
Super luminous dial
Antishock and antimagnetic**

Use box for cigarettes after removing this card and watch support

ROLEX SUBMARINER
INSTRUCTION MANUAL REF. 6536

It is especially rare to find old watches accompanied by their original instruction manual.
Although today many collectors seek out watches with the original box and documentation,
with vintage watches this is less important. Nevertheless, their presence adds value.

SEA-DWELLER COMEX

ROLEX – 1967

From 1970 to 1997, Rolex worked closely with Comex and its divers so that it could perfect its techniques and models. Rolex Comex watches were the precursors of modern dive watches. They were made in limited numbers, and today they drive the collectors' market wild.

SEE OPPOSITE	1977 MODEL
MANUFACTURER	ROLEX
MODEL	SEA-DWELLER COMEX
REFERENCE	1665
DIAL	BLACK
WINDING MECHANISM	AUTOMATIC
CALIBRE	1570
DIAMETER	40MM
MATERIAL	STEEL
STRAP	RUBBER
TYPE	TROPIC 66

ROLEX SUBMARINER COMEX

1970-1973	SUBMARINER 5513 (VH)
1972-1978	SUBMARINER 5514 (VH)
1978-1979	SUBMARINER 1680 (WITHOUT VH)
1982-1986	SUBMARINER 16800 (WITHOUT VH)
1988-1989	SUBMARINER 168000 (WITHOUT VH)
1986-1997	SUBMARINER 16610 (WITHOUT VH)

ROLEX SEA-DWELLER COMEX

1977-1980	SEA-DWELLER 1665 (VH)
1980-1984	SEA-DWELLER 16660 (VH)
1992-1997	SEA-DWELLER 16600 (VH)

HELIUM RELEASE VALVE

The Submariner went on sale in 1954. A year later the model was upgraded and made waterproof to 200m. Despite everything, this depth proved to be insufficient for professionals. In 1967, Rolex launched the Sea-Dweller (ref. 1665), which was waterproof to 600m and one of the first watches (along with the Doxa Sub, see page 154) to feature a helium release valve. At the time, deep dives were catastrophic for watches, especially when they were returned to the surface in a hyperbaric decompression chamber. In such a chamber, divers breathe a mixture of air, helium and hydrogen. When helium atoms penetrate the joints of a watch case, the difference in pressure causes the glass to come off or burst. The valve, which allows the gas to be progressively removed while preventing water from entering the watch, was therefore a major advance in the design of dive models. In order to test its watches, Rolex approached Comex (Compagnie Maritime d'Expertises), a French company based in Marseille that specializes in engineering and subsea work and was founded by Henri Delauze in 1962. The relationship between the two companies lasted 27 years, from 1970 to 1997, and Rolex produced nine models of the Submariner and Sea-Dweller exclusively for Comex that never went on sale.

SUBMARINER AND SEA-DWELLER

The first watch Rolex created for Comex dates from 1970. It was a Submariner, ref. 5513, and featured a helium release valve. Development continued with another Submariner that also featured a valve, the ref. 5514, of which 154 were made exclusively for Comex. Between 1978 and 1997, Rolex produced other Submariners for the company, but these no longer featured the helium release valve, which was now reserved for the Sea-Dweller models: ref. 1680, 16800, 168000 and 16610. The first Sea-Dweller Comex, ref. 1665, appeared in 1977. About 300 watches were made for the company's divers until 1980. From 1980 to 1984, they were equipped with ref. 16660 watches, waterproof to 600m. From 1992 to 1997, these were improved with ref. 16600, now waterproof to 1,220m. None of the Submariners and Sea-Dwellers bearing the Comex stamp went on general sale, and all were made in limited numbers. Specific features were used to differentiate the Comex Rolexes from those meant for the public: the first Comex examples had a discreet mark on the back, and some time later the dials sported a signature that has become legendary. Also, the caseback was engraved with a number, allowing Comex to keep a register of which watch was allocated to which diver.

SUBMARINER

TUDOR – 1954

**The first Tudor Submariner was created in 1954.
Tested by GERS (Groupe d'études et de recherches sous-marines) in 1956,
it was used by units of the French navy.**

MANUFACTURER	TUDOR

1. SEE OPPOSITE AND OVERLEAF, LEFT

MODEL	OYSTER PRINCE SUBMARINER SNOWFLAKE M.N. (MARINE NATIONALE (FRENCH NAVY) 1975
REFERENCE	9401
DIAL	BLUE
WINDING MECHANISM	AUTOMATIC
CALIBRE	2776
DIAMETER	40MM
MATERIAL	STEEL
STRAP	N/A
TYPE	N/A

2. SEE OVERLEAF, RIGHT

MODEL	PRINCE OYSTERDATE SUBMARINER TRANSITIONAL 1985
REFERENCE	76100
DIAL	BLUE
WINDING MECHANICM	AUTOMATIC
CALIBRE	2824-2
DIAMETER	40MM
MATIERIAL	STEEL
STRAP	STEEL
TYPE	OYSTER

DEVELOPMENT WITH THE GERS GROUP

During the 1950s, Tudor developed a series of dive watches aimed at professionals. The ref. 7922, bearing the name Oyster Prince Submariner, was unveiled in 1954. It was given specific features that were geared to its function: a case with a screwed back and screw-down crown that was waterproof to 100m, a dial that was readable in deep water, Mercedes hands (see page 22) and a graduated bidirectional bezel. The following year the manufacturer offered the ref. 7923, which was thinner thanks to its mechanical winding mechanism. In 1956 the subsea study and research group GERS, based in Toulon, tested both. Its commanding officer pronounced the waterproofing 'perfect' and the performance 'completely correct', but placed a new order for watches waterproof to 200m. Accordingly, in 1958 the ref. 7924, renamed Big Crown by enthusiasts, appeared. It was so-called because, as well as a thick case, it had a large screw-down crown. The model evolved in the following year when Tudor introduced a crown gaurd with ref. 7928. The shape of the case protected the crown, a development which delighted divers, especially those from the French navy.

THE FRENCH NAVY

The second era of the Submariner began in 1969, when the movements used in the watches (Fleurier calibres) were replaced by ETA automatic movements. When it came to the look of the watch, the logo featuring a rose was replaced by a shield.

The ref. 7016 (without date) and 7021 (with date) in particular moved away from the Rolex style, with a combination of square, luminous indexes and angular hands nicknamed Snowflake. The improved readability was appreciated by the French navy, which adopted the watch from 1974. In 1975, Tudor perfected the model with the ref. 9401 (without date) and 9411 (with date), both of which fitted with a movement with an improved performance. Once again, the version with a blue dial and hands was chosen by the French armed forces. Engraved with the initials M N followed by the year of supply on the back, the Snowflakes delivered to the navy until the 1980s are much sought after by collectors today.

VERSIONS AND HERITAGE

In around 1984, a transitional reference, the 76100, appeared. It was technically similar to the previous generation but the design of the dial and hands had been altered. Available only with a date function, it was referred to as Lollipop on account of the shape of the hour hand. The penultimate generation, ref. 79090, came out in 1989 and marked a return to Mercedes hands. The last, ref. 79190, appeared in the catalogue in 1995 and included developments such as a sapphire glass and a notched unidirectional rotating bezel. In 2012, at Baselworld, Tudor modernized the model with the Black Bay range, which reintroduced some design features of the first watches. That same year, Snowflake hands made a comeback in the Pelagos range.

SEAMASTER 600 'PLOPROF'

OMEGA – 1971

In 1971, after a series of tests and a few prototypes, the Seamaster 600 went on sale. Because it was aimed at professional divers, it was dubbed the Ploprof.

SEE OPPOSITE	1972 MODEL
MANUFACTURER	OMEGA
MODEL	SEAMASTER 600 'PLOPROF'
REFERENCE	166.077
DIAL	BLUE
WINDING MECHANISM	AUTOMATIC
CALIBRE	1002
DIAMETER	45 × 55MM
MATERIAL	STEEL
STRAP	STEEL
TYPE	SHARK (MILANESE MESH)

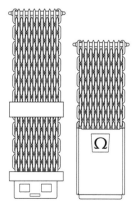

OMEGA
SHARK STRAP

During the 1970s, Omega offered customers a Milanese mesh strap, known as Shark, for its Ploprof model. Divers could use a rubber extension to lengthen it.

AIMED AT PROFESSIONALS

After World War II, diving was revolutionized following the perfection of the design for compressed air cylinders and diving mechanisms. In this climate, watch manufacturers vied with each other to create imaginative solutions for evermore waterproof watches. Rather than evolving the Seamaster 300, which had been in its catalogue since 1957 (see page 146), Omega started to develop a new range aimed specifically at professional divers. The man behind this idea was none other than Frédéric Robert, former boss of Aquastar (see page 152), who had been an adviser to Omega since 1967 (see page 118). After a series of tests and some prototypes, the Seamaster 600 (ref. 166.077) went on sale in 1971. Another watch, the ref. 166.093 Seamaster 1,000m, was introduced the following year, and offered for sale to the general public from 1976. Only the first of these was named Ploprof, even though the second, dubbed La Grande (The Big One), was also aimed at professionals.

FEATURES

The Ploprof stood out from its competitors thanks to its revolutionary feature, which prevented any water penetration and protected divers from making any accidental manoeuvres. The watch, which had no screwed caseback or helium release valve (see page 154), featured a case (CH480680) made out of a single piece of Uranus steel, which was highly resistant to corrosion. The case was granted a patent in 1967.

The glass on the Ploprof was pressed at 120kg and, held in place on the seal by a ring. The crown – screw-down, naturally – was on the left and protected by a locking nut, also patented (CH503310). One element stood out: the red button that unlocked the bidirectional bezel. On its release the Ploprof, which cost as much as two Submariners, was available with Isofrane (rubber) straps in four colours, as well as an optional steel strap. Another, in Milanese mesh, known as Shark, appeared in the mid-1970s. These early versions were fitted with automatic calibres (cal. 1000/1002) and were made with several styles of dial and bezel.

COMEX AND ICONIC STATUS

From 1968, before the watch went on sale in 1971, the prototypes were tested by Comex (see page 138). As part of these tests, three divers on the Janus II mission were equipped with the watch. They wore it for four hours each day for a week, at a depth of 253m, in the Gulf of Ajaccio. Certain models were also sent to the Ocean Systems Inc. research centre in the United States. The company said that they were 'more waterproof than a submarine'. In fact, although it was declared to be waterproof to 600m, the watch proved to be waterproof to a depth of 1,370m, stopping only when the glass, deformed by pressure, compressed the hands. Produced in small numbers and extremely expensive, the Ploprof was highly appreciated by some members of Captain Cousteau's crew. However, it was a captain of industry, Gianni Agnelli, who exported it beyond the seas.

SEAMASTER 300

OMEGA – 1957

In 1957, at the same time as the Speedmaster and Railmaster, Omega launched the Seamaster 300 – a dive watch aimed at professionals. Since 2014, Omega has offered new versions of the watch, inspired by the original design and incorporating the latest technical innovations.

SEE OPPOSITE	1963 MODEL
MANUFACTURER	OMEGA
MODEL	SEAMASTER 300
REFERENCE	ST 165.014
DIAL	BLACK
WINDING MECHANISM	AUTOMATIC
CALIBRE	552
DIAMETER	39MM
MATERIAL	STEEL
STRAP	N/A
TYPE	N/A

OMEGA'S PROFESSIONAL DIVE WATCH

Omega had been renowned for its waterproof watches since it created the Marine and Seamaster models (see page 58). But faced with competition from Blancpain and Rolex (see pages 132 and 134) it decided to position itself on the professional diving market. Rolex had patented a screw-down crown, so Omega developed its own system, the Naiad. It worked on a principle not unlike that of the Super Compressor watches (see page 148): the greater the water pressure, the more the crown was compressed. It was later established that this system was effective at great depths, but less so at shallow ones. The dial on these professional models featured the figure 300, a reference to the watch's waterproofing, to distinguish them from other designs. However, due to the technical capacities of measuring instruments at the time, this Seamaster was only tested to 200m.

EVOLUTION

The watch was waterproof, automatic and featured a bidirectional bezel, as well as a dial with large, luminous indexes. Between its launch and the 1970s, several generations of the watch followed, each containing sub-references. From 1957 to 1961, the CK 2913 (-1 to -8) models were fitted with 500/501 calibres. They featured a 39mm symmetrical case with straight lugs and Broad Arrow (-1 to -5) or dauphine (-4 to -8) hands (see page 22). The CK14755 models were sold from 1961 to 1963. They were similar to the previous generations, but fitted with movements that performed better – calibres 550/552.

Baton hands and new typography characterized the transitional references ST 165.014, which again had straight lugs. They appeared in around 1963 and were available until 1967. The real change came with the ST 165.024, which was produced from 1963, offered in a Date version from 1968 and was available until 1971. It featured a 40mm asymmetrical case, whose main function was to protect the crown. During its production, a new shape of hour hand, called Sword, appeared, and a few rare dials, which were also designed for the British army, sported an oversized triangle dubbed Big Triangle.

COLLABORATION AND HERITAGE

During the 1960s, Seamaster 300 watches became the first choice for experienced divers. Certain Big Triangle military models with a fixed spring bar welded to the case were made especially for the Special Boat Service, a special forces unit of the British Royal Navy. Likewise, Captain Cousteau's crew used them on the Précontinent II project. These watches also proved their worth with Comex, and were tested during the Physalie experiments on the Janus operation. The model fell off the radar until 1993, when Omega launched the Seamaster Diver 300m, the design of which differed from that of its illustrious forebears. The 1995 James Bond movie *GoldenEye* did much for the Diver 300m model's popularity and highlighted a partnership, still in existence today, between the world's most famous secret agent and the Seamaster 300.

SUPER COMPRESSOR

WITTNAUER – 1960

During the 1960s, many watch manufacturers fitted their dive watches with Super Compressor cases, an invention patented by the company belonging to Ervin Piquerez.

SEE OPPOSITE	**1960 MODEL**
MANUFACTURER	**WITTNAUER**
MODEL	**SCUBA-MATIC**
REFERENCE	**8007**
DIAL	**BLACK**
WINDING MECHANISM	**AUTOMATIC**
CALIBRE	**C11 KAS-1**
DIAMETER	**36MM**
MATERIAL	**STEEL**
STRAP	**LEATHER**
TYPE	**SIMPLE**

THE INVENTOR OF COMPRESSOR CASES

Super Compressor is not the name of a model or a make of watch. The term denotes a type of case used during the 1960s by numerous watch manufacturers for their dive watches. During that decade Ervin Piquerez, from the Bernese Jura in Switzerland, was the main case manufacturer. In 1953, Piquerez SA (EPSA) registered patents for the manufacture of a revolutionary system. The company had developed a concept that consisted of increasing the waterproofing of a watch as the depth of water increased: the deeper underwater the watch was, the greater the pressure exerted on the caseback, and the more the toric joint was compressed. The most iconic cases were certainly those with two crowns, but EPSA made them with one, or three, like the one manufactured for the Jaeger-LeCoultre Memovox Polaris (see page 174). Regardless of the make of the watch using the case, these crowns were often square and did not always bear a logo.

MODELS WITH TWO CROWNS

The bezel is of crucial importance during a dive. In order to calculate the time spent underwater, the diver aligns the bezel's zero marker with the minute hand. In order to avoid any accidental change, some high-end models feature a unidirectional bezel; other, later examples, a locking nut (see page 144). Super Compressor watches use another system to protect the bezel, by locating it under the glass. This internal bezel can be rotated using the first crown, located at 2 o'clock. The second, located at 4 o'clock, allows the time to be adjusted and, on some models, the date. These are easy to recognize, and the size differs noticeably between different models. The inside or outside of the backs of the cases are generally engraved with the EPSA logo – the image of a diver. Although most models are 36mm in size, there are bigger ones, like the Longines ref. 7042-1, which measures 42mm.

A UNIVERSALLY POPULAR CASE

It is impossible to make a list of the exact number of makes that used these cases. Some collectors have counted more than one hundred. Here is a non-exhaustive list: Universal Genève, Longines, Jaeger-LeCoultre, Hamilton, LIP, but also Bulova, with its Explorer dial, Enicar (in its military or GMT version, see page 164) and the Wittnauer Scuba-Matic. These many partnerships enabled EPSA to grow rapidly until the beginning of the 1970s. Although its turnover was more than £2.7 million (25 million francs), and some 500 people were employed by the company, this momentum ground to a halt with the death of its founder in 1971. In 2007, Longines relaunched its Super Compressor model, unchanged, with the Legend Diver. Today, many manufacturers wisely use the rotating inner bezel designs created by Ervin Piquerez to give their dive watches style.

STRAPS

FACT SHEET N°13

Every watch is sold with at least one strap, sometimes two
for certain dive models. Despite this, enthusiasts like to
personalize their watches.

LEATHER

This is the traditional material for making watch straps. Making a leather strap involves several operations, often carried out by hand. The finishing touches are important, but so is the source of the leather. Several kinds are popular: alligator for its firmness and texture, calfskin for its strength and comfort, and Shell Cordovan, a supple horse leather famous for its use in boot making. If you wear a leather strap daily, the acidity of your skin and the weather will change it. Today, vegan straps are used to imitate leather.

METAL

These straps take the form of linked chains and are a minutely detailed assembly of dozens of components. Not all of the parts are visible and some play a decorative rather than a functional role. Until the beginning of the 20th century, pocket watches were attached to chains. As the wristwatch became popular, companies that manufactured watch chains had to adapt. Gay Frères managed this transition, and the biggest watchmakers of the time soon became its customers. The company is therefore responsible for the Oyster strap, certain *grain de riz* (rice grain) straps, and some Bamboo ones inspired by the Bonklip design. As with watches, several materials are used (such as steel and gold), and many forms exist (Milanese mesh, mesh, jubilee and so on).

RUBBER

In the 1960s, during the heyday of the dive watch, it became evident that these watches required straps that were flexible, strong, comfortable and waterproof. At the time, most watches were sold with metal straps which were not ideal when worn for diving. Professional divers used leather or fabric straps, which quickly deteriorated on contact with salt water. Watchmakers, rather than manufacturers, then suggested a third option: Tropic straps. Little is known of the inventor of these straps, but it is believed that it was Bollier SA, a company based in Bienne, Switzerland. The success of this design led to manufacturers including Omega, Enicar, Nivada, Blancpain and Yema fitting their dive watches with Tropic straps as standard. The straps were made from a natural, vulcanized, hypoallergenic rubber using a unique process: a vulcanizing agent (generally sulphur) was added to an unprocessed elastomer and these were then heated, which resulted in links forming between the chain molecules. In short, this process rendered the material less plastic, more elastic and therefore stronger. Although the straps were primarily used for diving, they were also sold for other uses. Among the many designs of Tropic strap, that were advertised were the 'Tropic 66, the ideal strap for dive watches'; 'Tropic Star, the elegant strap'; and 'Tropic Sport, the GT strap for the sportsman'.

Some 10 years later, the ISOfrane strap appeared. It was made of isoprene and was used for the Ploprof (see page 144).

NATO

Highly fashionable, the acronym Nato indicated that the strap was listed in the stock of the North Atlantic Treaty Organisation. Although initially intended for use by the military, thanks to its ease of use it crossed a boundary and was adopted for civilian use. This is different from a Zulu strap, which is aesthetically similar but doesn't have the extra material underneath the watch that is designed to stop it from slipping off the wrist.

BUCKLE

The buckle is indispensable as it joins the two ends of the strap. The oldest and most common type is the pin buckle, which sometimes bears the manufacturer's logo. The folding clasp, which is found on both Cartier and dive watches, is a system that secures the strap by locking. This hinged buckle unfolds when the strap is undone. It is opened and closed using a push-button. If it opens accidentally, the watch does not fall off but remains on the wrist. A deployant clasp combines both the folding clasp and pin-buckle so that it's both easy to put on and easy to adjust.

ROLEX
OYSTER STRAP

OMEGA
FLAT LINK STRAP

ROLEX
JUBILEE STRAP

FORSTNER
JB CHAMPION

FOLDING CLASP

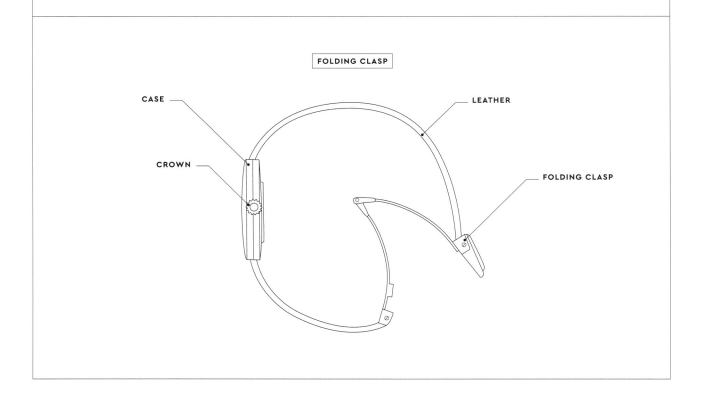

CASE

LEATHER

CROWN

FOLDING CLASP

AIRSTAR

JEANRICHARD – 1962

Aquastar, formerly JeanRichard, was a 1960s brand founded by Frédéric Robert that was exclusively devoted to water sports. It was one of the first companies to offer chronographs for diving.

SEE OPPOSITE	**1962 MODEL**
MANUFACTURER	**JEANRICHARD**
MODEL	**AIRSTAR**
REFERENCE	**905 182**
DIAL	**BLACK**
WINDING MECHANISM	**MECHANICAL**
CALIBRE	**VALJOUX 72**
DIAMETER	**38MM**
MATERIAL	**STEEL**
STRAP	**RUBBER**
TYPE	**TROPIC 66**

AQUASTAR
DEEPSTAR

The Aquastar Deepstar features an exclusive bezel, patented in 1964, which allows divers to perform no fewer than five calculations.

FRÉDÉRIC ROBERT AND AQUASTAR

Aquastar was founded by Frédéric Robert, a businessman, sailor and diver, who wanted to develop water sports instruments. In 1962, he took charge of the JeanRichard company, which was founded by his father and had just registered two patents: one for a measuring instrument for diving, featuring a rotating bezel, and another for a regatta watch. That year, a patent for an internal rotating bezel was registered. The first models bore the name JeanRichard, but this was changed to Aquastar, to reflect the make's identity. Unlike its competitors, Aquastar concentrated exclusively on the water sports sector. Gradually, it attracted elite divers, such as Jacques Mayol, who wore a Benthos 500 when he set his freediving record. As true diving instruments, Aquastar's products were available only through specialist sales outlets, such as Scubapro in the United States, Spirotechnique in France and Nemrod in Spain.

AQUASTAR CHRONOGRAPHS

Aquastar was one of the first manufacturers to offer chronographs for diving, at a time when such watches were normally confined to motor racing and aviation (see pages 71 and 105). Two models appeared during the 1960s: the Deepstar, waterproof to 100m, and the mysterious Airstar, waterproof to a more modest 20m. The former stood out thanks to its exclusive bezel, which was patented in 1964, and allowed five calculations to be made: total dive time, speed of ascent, decompression time, nitrogen desaturation and increase in the duration of stages in the event of successive dives. This chronograph, which featured a readable dial with a large counter at 3 o'clock, was used on board the *Calypso*, along with the Seamaster 300 (see page 146), Doxa (see page 154) and the Submariner (see pages 134 and 140). The other model, the Airstar, was made in small numbers (about 200) and featured the prestigious Valjoux 72 (see page 79). It appeared initially under the name JeanRichard, without a model name. Airstar appeared on the dial of a transitional model, associated with JeanRichard but featuring a crown bearing the name Aquastar. It became Aquastar Airstar when the company changed its name, but it appears never to have gone on sale. The examples that have been found are often in excellent condition, some are even new-old stock, which seems surprising for a professional watch.

AQUASTAR'S RESURRECTION

In 1974, Frédéric Robert left Aquastar and joined Omega as an adviser. In 1975, the company was sold to the EREN Group, which subsequently sold it to Frères Seinet in 1982. However, in order to survive, Aquastar had no choice but to offer customers quartz or LED watches. Rick Marei, a dive watch enthusiast who was behind the resurrection of Doxa and Tropic, convinced Marc Seinet to relaunch Aquastar. The latter ended up selling the business to the Synchron group, owned by Marei. In 2020, Marei's first action was to successfully relaunch the Deepstar, this time with an automatic movement.

SUB 300T

DOXA - 1967

In 1967, the Doxa Sub was unveiled.
This watch, with its iconic orange dial, was aimed at the general public but its features
meant that is also appealed to professionals. Although Doxa had a low profile
for some decades, in 2019 it started to make a big comeback.

SEE OPPOSITE	1970 MODEL
MANUFACTURER	DOXA
MODEL	SUB 300T
REFERENCE	N/A
DIAL	ORANGE
WINDING MECHANISM	AUTOMATIC
CALIBRE	ETA 2783
DIAMETER	42MM
MATERIAL	STEEL
STRAP	N/A
TYPE	N/A

DOXA
HELIUM RELEASE VALVE

In 1969, Doxa developed the helium
release valve – a system that allowed a
watch to withstand pressure better.

A DIVE WATCH FOR EVERYONE

In 1889, Georges Ducommun built the Doxa factory in Le Locle, Switzerland. The company designed pocket watches and then, thanks to its patented 8 Days calibre, specialized in on-board instruments that were fitted to the first Bugattis. However, the firm had its moment of glory in the 1960s thanks to the world of diving. In 1964, when specialized watches were aimed at professionals, Urs Eschle, who was in charge of development at Doxa, produced a reliable, accessible watch aimed at the general public. Indeed, Georges Ducommun's mantra had always been to offer 'a high-quality watch at a reasonable price'. He therefore set up a team of professional divers to design the ideal watch.

DIVE WATCH

After three years' research, the Doxa Sub was unveiled at Baselworld and it went on sale in 1967. Everything was geared to making the watch a true dive tool (see page 131). The wide steel case protected the screw-down crown and made the watch waterproof to 300m. It boasted a patented external unidirectional bezel with two distinct scales: an orange one on the outer 'depth' ring and a black one on the inner 'minutes' ring. It was inspired by the US Navy's no-decompression diving table, which allowed divers to monitor their dive time based on depth in order to ensure a safe return to the surface. The Sub 300 was sold with a metal strap featuring a pawl system that was integrated with the clasp and made it easier to put on over a wetsuit. The dial featured luminous indexes and hands.

The minute hand was broader, since it is the one divers use to calculate their sessions. But the special feature of the Doxa was undoubtedly the orange colour of its dial. Tests showed that it offered optimum visibility, even at a depth of 30m. This model, initially designed with the wider public in mind, quickly won over professionals. Jacques Cousteau even secured exclusive distribution rights for his American company, US Divers, which sold models adorned with an Aqua Lung logo.

ORANGE MANIA

This success drove the Swiss teams to perfect their concept. When they are in a decompression chamber at a great depth, divers breathe a mixture of air, helium and hydrogen. But when helium atoms penetrate the joints in the case of a watch, the pressure difference causes the glass to be blown off. Doxa, in collaboration with Rolex, patented a valve system: the helium release valve. It was first used in 1969 on the Sub 300T Conquistador, which featured on the wrist of Robert Redford in the movie *Three Days of the Condor*. In the mid-1960s, an incredible wave of orange engulfed the market. The watch appealed to the general public after it was seen on television being worn by divers in the Cousteau crew, and also thanks to the novels written by Clive Cussler, whose main character Dirk Pitt wears a Doxa.

COMPLICATIONS

CHAPTER 4

SIMPLE

COMPLICATIONS

On a watch, a complication is any function
other than the display of hours, minutes
and seconds.

FUNCTIONS AND COMPLICATIONS

At a very minimum, a watch displays the hours and minutes, but it can offer much more than that. The term 'complication' denotes any display other than the hours and minutes that is connected to the measurement of time, regardless of how the watch is rewound (manually or automatically). Modules are added to the watch's movement. In addition, there are complex mechanisms that are unconnected to the measurement of time, such as the power reserve and tourbillons. The power reserve is the length of time the movement functions when its mainspring is wound to the maximum. When the power reserve is exhausted, the mechanism ceases to function and the watch stops. Some watches indicate the amount of energy remaining in the movement through an aperture. The tourbillon is a device that was perfected by Abraham-Louis Breguet in 1801. It was designed to compensate for disturbances to the running of the movement caused by the earth's gravitational field. The components of this type of movement are contained in a small mobile cage, located in the centre of the watch; a movement like this is the preserve of a few exceptional craftsmen. Even though it is not a strict distinction, this book will differentiate between simple complications and more advanced ones (see page 171). Supplementary functions, such as protection from magnetic fields or the indication of time zones by means of the bezel, are also explained.

SIMPLE COMPLICATIONS

Date/day: as the name suggests, this complication displays the date and day of the week. Watches with a simple calendar (or simple date) display the date, without allowing for the difference in the length of months. They must therefore be adjusted manually five times a year. The display of the date may be complemented by the indication of the day, month or even phase of the moon (triple calendar).

GMT: the GMT (Greenwich Mean Time) function, which is of particular interest to travellers, displays the time in at least two time zones – local time and reference time (the time in one's place of residence, for example). A GMT watch is operated via a combination of adjusting a fourth hand (generally shaped like an arrow) and the use of an internal or external bidirectional bezel.

World time: this refers to watches that indicate local time (real solar time) in several world cities, often chosen in light of their political or economic importance. On a world time watch, a ring displays the cities that represent the 24 time zones. Depending on the model, this ring can be turned by adjusting the crown or a small push-button. Some watches simply have an external bezel that is adjusted manually.

Chronograph: at the beginning of the 20th century the first single push-button wrist chronographs appeared. These required a high level of expertise as the three functions (start, stop and zero) are activated using a single push-button. In 1933, Breitling developed the first wrist chronograph with two push-buttons, of which one served simply to reset the second hand to zero, making the operation of the watch simpler. It allows a short period of time to be measured independently of the watch's other displays. The chronograph hand can be started, stopped and reset to zero according to the interval of time to be measured.

Stop seconds: this system enables the watch to be synchronized with the actual time. This complication stops the second hand when the crown is pulled.

Antimagnetic: this is a watch designed to avoid the effects of magnetism. It should be stressed that this is not a complication in the strict sense of the term, since it does not involve the movement, but instead it is protected by a Faraday cage.

Rotating bezel: this is especially important for models designed for diving. It cannot be considered a complication because it is not part of the movement, but it can take on a role that adds a function to the watch, such as the measuring the length of time of a dive.

MILGAUSS

ROLEX - 1956

**In the mid-1950s, Rolex added the Milgauss to its range.
This professional watch, tested by scientists,
is unaffected by magnetic fields.**

SEE OPPOSITE	**1968 MODEL**
MANUFACTURER	**ROLEX**
MODEL	**MILGAUSS**
REFERENCE	**1019**
DIAL	**SILVER, LUMINOUS**
WINDING MECHANISM	**AUTOMATIC**
CALIBRE	**1580**
DIAMETER	**38MM**
MATERIAL	**STEEL**
STRAP	**STEEL**
TYPE	**OYSTER**

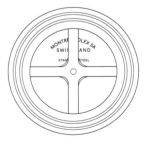

**ROLEX
1019 MAIN PLATE**

Resistance to magnetic fields is made possible by
a mild steel cage known as a Faraday cage.
Rolex complemented this protection with a
special X-shaped main plate.

FARADAY CAGE

In the mid-1950s, after the Explorer and
Submariner (see pages 54 and 134), which
had been designed for climbers and divers
respectively, Rolex launched a model
aimed at scientists. These experts were not
contending with the pressure of the depths
of the ocean, but with magnetic fields, which
are measured in gauss. These caused the
balance to malfunction or stop as soon as the
threshold of 50–100 G was crossed. In 1954,
Rolex teamed up with Conseil Européen pour
la Recherche Nucléaire (CERN, the European
organization for nuclear research) to create a
watch that withstood 1,000 G, aptly named
the Milgauss, by protecting the movement
with a Faraday cage – a mild steel cage that
is resistant to magnetism and located inside
the watch case.

FIRST GENERATIONS

In 1952, two years before it went on general
sale, ref. 6543 was tested by researchers. It
is believed that fewer than 200 of this model
were made over a short period of time. The
watch featured a 38mm case without a crown
guard, and a rotating bezel. The dial had a
honeycomb texture, and it had dauphine-type
(see page 22) hour and minute hands. This
first series was fine-tuned when it entered
the company's catalogue in 1956, with the
similar ref. 6541. However, it had a new
feature, which would become the signature
of contemporary models: a second hand
shaped like a bolt of lightning. Production
only lasted for four years because of its
limited popularity. Some watches made
for the American market replaced the
rotating bezel with a smooth one.

In 1960, the Milgauss got a new look with
the ref. 1019. The rotating bezel was replaced
with a smooth one, and the lightning
bolt second hand was replaced with a
conventional one. As for the dial, it lost its
textured look and – a novelty for Rolex –
three variations were made: black, silver
with luminous indexes (made of tritium) and
silver without luminous indexes. This last
version was a response to a recommendation
by CERN. In fact, the radioactivity of
tritium, although less hazardous than that of
the radium which had been used previously,
interfered with equipment being used. The
models without tritium used by CERN are
among the most sought-after by collectors.

REVIVAL

In 2007, Baselworld sprang a surprise when
it gave the Milgauss a new life with the
reference 116400GV (standing for *glace
verte* – French for 'green glass'. Indeed, the
manufacturer had fitted this model with
a green sapphire glass that was almost
impossible to scratch. Because it was
extremely difficult to manufacture, it had
not bothered to register a patent for the
glass. The Milgauss, the case of which had
increased in size to 40mm, featured a calibre
3131 and became the first watch resistant to
magnetic fields to be certified by the Contrôle
Officiel Suisse des Chronomètres (COSC, the
official Swiss chronometer testing institute).
As regards design, it combined the best
features of its forerunners: a smooth bezel
like the ref. 1019 and a lightning bolt second
hand like the ref. 6241.

GMT MASTER

ROLEX – 1954

In the mid-1950s, Rolex created the legendary Pepsi, a watch that could display a second time zone
for pilots of Pan American World Airways, the airline known as Pan Am.
In 2007, the iconic bezel was no longer used for steel models.
Rolex put that right 11 years later.

SEE OPPOSITE	1957 MODEL
MANUFACTURER	ROLEX
MODEL	GMT MASTER
REFERENCE	6542
DIAL	LACQUERED (GILT) TROPICAL
WINDING MECHANISM	AUTOMATIC
CALIBRE	1065
DIAMETER	38MM
MATERIAL	STEEL
STRAP	STEEL
TYPE	JUBILEE

GMT MASTER

1954	6542
1959	1675
1980	16750
1988	16700

GMT MASTER II

1983	16760
1989	16710
2007	116710
2018	126710

A SECOND TIME ZONE

During the 1950s, Pan Am, one of the biggest companies at the time, was searching for a watch for its pilots that could simultaneously display the local time and the time at their home base. Rolex developed a watch with two time zones for its fleet: the GMT Master (a reference to Greenwich Mean Time). At that time, pilots used universal time as a reference point. Rolex gave its new creation a 24-hour calibrated rotating bezel and a fourth hand. To use it, all the pilot needed to do was to pull on the crown and set the hour and minute hands; the new GMT hand followed them. In this way, it was possible to display the time in a second time zone simply by turning the bezel.

PEPSI

The term Pepsi is often used for this watch because the colours of each half of the bezel recall the visual identity of the fizzy drink. From a technical point of view, blue indicated the night hours, and red the daytime hours. The ref. 6542 appeared in 1954 and continued until 1959. This automatic watch, which was waterproof to 50m, inherited some features of the Submariner (see page 134), notably the rotating bezel, but this time with a 24-hour scale. On the early versions Bakelite was used, but this was replaced by aluminium. The hour hand was of the Mercedes shape and the GMT hand was red with an arrow at its end. The watch had a date with Cyclops lens and a 38mm case without a crown guard. In 1959, the ref. 1675 was introduced and remained in the catalogue until 1980.

Also automatic, it benefited from a better-performing calibre, the 1565, which was replaced by the 1575. The size of the waterproof case had been increased to 40mm, and the crown was now protected by a crown guard. As regards design, this reference laid the foundations for future GMT watches. In 1981, the model evolved with the ref. 16750, which was now waterproof to 100m and featured the 3075 calibre, which offered a quickset date feature.

GMT MASTER II

In 1983, Rolex unveiled the GMT Master II ref. 16760. Despite the release of this watch, the GMT Master I was still available with the ref. 16700 and it replaced the 16750 in 1988. Named as Fat Lady on account of its wide case, it featured a new function that made it possible to read a third time zone: the calibre 3085, which made the fourth hand independent. The central hands displayed the local time; the GMT hand moved independently and pointed at the 24-hour bezel for a second time zone; and the rotating bezel made it possible to give the time in a third time zone. In 1983, a new variant, nicknamed Coke, featured a red and black bezel. In 1989, ref. 16710 saw tritium replaced by luminova. There are three bezel configurations available on the steel models ref. 126710: blue/black, nicknamed Batman (appeared in 2007 on ref. 116710); green/black, dubbed Sprite; and, naturally, the Pepsi.

SHERPA GUIDE

ENICAR – 1960

**The Sherpa Guide is a distillation of Enicar's expertise.
It brings together a Super Compressor case, a GMT function and a World Time external bezel,
all of which had been developed for other models made by the manufacturer.**

SEE OPPOSITE	1963 MODEL
MANUFACTURER	ENICAR
MODEL	SHERPA GUIDE
REFERENCE	146/001
DIAL	SILVER
WINDING MECHANISM	AUTOMATIC
CALIBRE	AR1146
DIAMETER	42MM
MATERIAL	STEEL
STRAP	LEATHER
TYPE	SIMPLE

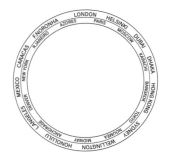

ENICAR
WORLD TIME BEZEL

A bezel featuring the names of
the world's major cities. The time
in these cities can be checked by
turning the bezel manually.

THE SHERPA RANGE

On 18 May 1956, the summits of Lhotse
and Mount Everest were reached by an
expedition whose members were equipped
with a waterproof Enicar watch, probably a
Seapearl. The manufacturer became front-
page news and, as Rolex did with its Explorer
(see page 54), seized the opportunity to use
this publicity. Consequently, a few months
later, it created the Sherpa range and its
numerous variants. At the time, Ariste
Racine was seeking to give the brand a boost
by giving it a sporty identity. The company
turned to the case manufacturer Piquerez
(see page 148) for most of the Sherpa models.
As a result, the range then comprised one
watch with date (Sherpa Date), a dive watch
(Sherpa Diver) and a GMT model (Sherpa
GMT), as well as a world time variant
(Sherpa World Time) that featured an
external bezel bearing the names of major
cities from around the world.

A DISTILLATION OF EXPERTISE

The Sherpa Guide model, which appeared
in 1960, was a distillation of all the
manufacturer's expertise. Besides the date,
Enicar combined three functions that had
been developed for some of its other models.
First, the watch was waterproof and featured
a Super Compressor case with two crowns.
As stated elsewhere, the deeper this type
of case went underwater, the greater the
pressure on the caseback, and the more the
toric joint was compressed. Subsequently,
like its Rolex counterpart that had been
released a few years earlier (see page 162)
and the single crown Sherpa, the Guide
offered a GMT function through its two-tone
internal bezel, calibrated with 24 hours,

and a fourth hand. Finally, the model
boasted an external World Time bezel.
When this was turned and positioned
with the fourth hand as a reference point,
it allowed the wearer to see the time in
different zones around the world. This
complication, featured widely on Enicar
models, was a variant of an invention by
the watchmaker Louis Cottier. The Sherpa
Guide, with its large diameter (42mm), is
often referred to as a true Swiss Army knife
among watches.

VARIANTS

There are many variants of the Sherpa
Guide. As is often the case with Enicar,
collectors classify the watches according to
the date of their release as Mark I, II, III
and IV. Largely manufactured during the
1960s, the first models featured dauphine
hands, which were replaced by baton hands
(see page 22). These watches were automatic,
and available with either a silver or black
dial. Changes to successive versions were
essentially made with the aim of improving
readability. The fourth hand was coloured
with a chequerboard pattern, as was the
internal GMT bezel, which over time became
yellow and a shade of orange. The chief
change concerned the shape of the case. It
featured long lugs with chamfers, but on the
Mark IV these were replaced by a tonneau-
shaped case (see page 20). These last models
coincided with Enicar's demise: the quartz
crisis (see page 209) dealt the company a
devastating blow and, despite a few attempts,
it never recovered.

DE VILLE DATO

OMEGA – 1967

First seen on the dial of Seamaster models, the inscription De Ville acquired an independent existence in 1967, when Omega decided to make it the name of a range of watches in its own right.

SEE OPPOSITE	**1969 MODEL**
MANUFACTURER	**OMEGA**
MODEL	**DE VILLE DATO**
REFERENCE	**146.017**
DIAL	**SILVER**
WINDING MECHANISM	**MECHANICAL**
CALIBRE	**930**
DIAMETER	**35MM**
MATERIAL	**STEEL**
STRAP	**LEATHER**
TYPE	**SIMPLE**

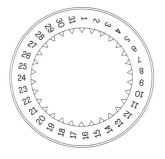

OMEGA
DATE DISC

The date disc turns under the dial and displays information through an aperture. The Omega De Ville Dato brings together the date complication and a chronograph.

INAUGURATION OF THE RANGE

The inscription De Ville first appeared on an Omega watch dial in 1963 as a category of the Seamaster (see page 58). Most of the time it featured three hands and was available in steel or as a gold-plated model. In 1967, Omega removed the word Seamaster from the name of the De Ville, making it a range of watches in its own right. This collection was positioned midway between the luxurious Constellation (see page 60) and the more sporty Seamaster and was therefore aimed at an elegant, city-dwelling clientele, hence its name. When it was launched, the models attracted public attention because of their Omega movements, exceptional finish and pared-back designs.

CHRONOGRAPH WITH DATE

Within the De Ville collection, the models with three hands met with great success, and some chronographs were also available. Among these was ref. 145.017, which was available in gold, gold-plated and steel versions, with a black or silver dial. The relative success of this model, which went somewhat unremarked at the time, led to its withdrawal from the catalogue after two years. This short production run makes the watch rare and it is now especially sought after by Omega collectors. The model, which boasts a modern design, features a 930 calibre. This is a modified version of the 861 calibre, itself a worthy successor to the prestigious 321 calibre (see page 100). It enables the watch to have a date disc, which is usually absent on 861 calibres. Here, the date is located at 9 o'clock. This recalls another chronograph of the time: the Heuer

Dato 45 ref. 3147 (see page 91). Unlike the latter, for which Heuer completely omitted a counter, Omega's idea was to place the date over the counter. The result is an original, functional design. Even though the second hand covers the date for an instant, the latter still remains very readable.

LEGACY

During the 1970s, the De Ville gained many plaudits. It won the Grand Prix Triomphe de l'Excellence Européenne (Grand Prize for European Excellence) and six Golden Roses at the Baden-Baden Design Awards. At the beginning of the 1990s, for the brand's 100th anniversary, Omega fitted a De Ville with a central tourbillon movement, a complex complication the purpose of which is to reduce the effect of gravity on the working of a mechanical watch. Dubbed Project 33 or P33, the development of this tourbillon was overseen by Moritz Grimm and André Beyner. This project was technically difficult to accomplish and was inspired by the Omega archives from the 1940s. Again, in 1999, the Omega De Ville was selected for a new development when it was fitted with the 2500 calibre, the brand's first coaxial escapement. Today the De Ville range is as elegant as ever and Omega continues to use it to highlight its cutting-edge technological innovations.

TRIPLE CALENDAR

WAKMANN – 1960

**Wakmann is an American brand that distributes Breitling in the USA.
Its most iconic creation, the Triple Calendar chronograph,
displays the day, month and date.**

SEE OPPOSITE	1960 MODEL
MANUFACTURER	WAKMANN
MODEL	TRIPLE CALENDAR
REFERENCE	71.1309.70
DIAL	REVERSE PANDA
WINDING MECHANISM	MECHANICAL
CALIBRE	723/72C
DIAMETER	37MM
MATERIAL	STEEL
STRAP	LEATHER
TYPE	RALLYE

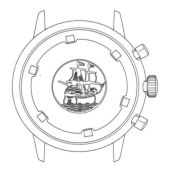

**WAKMANN
GALLEON ENGRAVING**

A galleon is engraved on the caseback of
Wakmann's Triple Calendar model.

SWISS WATCH IMPORT ACT

During World War II, Wakmann was based
in Portugal but at the end of the war, to
ensure it could continue to sell watches,
it moved to New York. As far as collectors
are concerned, the name Wakmann is
inseparable from Breitling. Like Wittnauer
for Longines (see page 96), Wakmann has
been the distributor for Breitling in the
United States since 1947. The reason for
this partnership lies in the Swiss Watch
Import Act. The American government
was committed to protecting its domestic
companies, whose production had been
impacted by the efforts made by their
Swiss competitors during the war. The law
prohibited the sale of watches that had
not been assembled in the US. Therefore
Wakmann, based on 47th Street in New York,
fitted a number of watches with movements
that had been made in Europe. Although
the Navitimer officially went on sale from
1954 (see page 106), it appears that from
1952 the first US Aircraft Owners and Pilots
Association (AOPA) watches were assembled
by Wakmann.

TRIPLE CALENDAR

The company's business model consisted
of distributing watches or fitting models
it had produced with prestigious Swiss
movements, such as Lemania (see page
101) or Valjoux (see page 79). Wakmann's
most iconic creation was undoubtedly the
Triple Calendar, which was fitted with the
723/72C, a derivative of the Valjoux 72.
This chronograph has three counters which,
unlike the standard version, displays a
triple date: the day and month are shown
in two windows at 12 o'clock, and the date

is indicated by a fourth, central hand that
points to an internal scale marked with
31 days. Steel and gold-plated versions of
the watch were available. The caseback
was usually engraved with a symbol that
represented the link between Wakmann and
Europe: a galleon – a 16th century sailing
ship that was used for trade.

A POPULAR COMPLICATION

The Valjoux 23 was developed by Reymond
Frères SA in 1916. The movement was
fitted with a column wheel and two push-
buttons. In 1929, John Reymond's brothers
Marius and Arnold took over the company,
which then became Valjoux SA. In 1946,
they launched the Valjoux series 70, 71, 72,
723/72C, 75, 76 and 77, which was based
on the Valjoux 23. Unlike the older model,
which drove chronographs with two counters,
this series drove chronographs with three
(see page 79). The calibre 723/72C (C for
'calendar'), which displayed a triple date,
was considered to be the company's flagship.
It was made until 1974, and used by big
brands such as Rolex and Heuer, but also by
more niche ones such as Gallet and Girard-
Perregaux. Although the ref. 6236, made
famous by the skier Jean-Claude Killy, can
fetch £550,000 ($700,000) at auction, it is
possible to find Triple Calendar models at far
more accessible prices.

ADVANCED

COMPLICATIONS

The number of additional components incorporated into a movement makes it possible to measure a watch's level of complication in a practical way.

ACOUSTIC COMPLICATIONS

Alarm: some watches have an alarm. When it is triggered, a hammer strikes until stored energy is exhausted or an automatic blocking system intervenes.

Sonnerie (or chime): a watch with a chime automatically chimes the passage of the hours and quarter-hours. The petite sonnerie (small chime) chimes the quarter-hours without repeating the hours and the grande sonnerie (big chime) repeats the hours when it chimes the quarter-hours.

Repeater: a watch with a repeater chimes the hour on demand. When a push-button or lock is pressed, the sound produced is different for hours, quarter-hours and minutes. This complication, derived from watches with a chime, is one of the most difficult to make.

SPLIT-TIME COUNTERS

Rattrapante (or split-seconds chronograph): this type of complex chronograph allows the measurement of several intermediate times. For example, you can register the times of two sprinters separately. In order to do this, the function has two superimposed second hands. When the chronograph starts, the two move in a synchronized manner. When the push-button is pressed, it stops the first hand while the second continues. A second push on the button stops the second hand. You can then read both times.

Mono-rattrapante (or flyback): this variant uses a single hand for lap timing and is less expensive to make. Generally, the upper push-button triggers the stop/ start function. If you then press the lower push-button, the hand stops and gives the intermediate time. Pressing the lower push-button a second time causes the hand to jump to where it would have been if it had not been stopped. There are several types of control for this function.

DATES AND ASTRONOMICAL DISPLAYS

Date: the simple date automatically displays the date by giving what day of the month it is. However, for months of less than 31 days, the date must be adjusted manually. The annual date does not take into account the month of February, or leap years, and must be adjusted manually once a year. The perpetual date function automatically takes into account regular and irregular (less than 31-day) months.

Moon phase: this complication displays the different phases of the moon over a complete cycle of about 29.5 days. It is not necessarily very useful, but has an aesthetic quality that is very popular. The most sophisticated moon phase is known as 'astronomical', which requires an adjustment of just one day every 122 years. The single most accurate moon phase is the Andreas Strehler Lune Exacte which only needs adjustment once every 2,060,757 years.

Once again, these complications can be combined. The more complications a watch has, the harder it will have been to manufacture.

CRICKET

VULCAIN – 1947

**In 1947, the first true wristwatch with an alarm
complication appeared. It was created by Vulcain.
Since its launch every US president has owned one.**

SEE OPPOSITE	1960 MODEL
MANUFACTURER	VULCAIN
MODEL	CRICKET, JUMBO
REFERENCE	303002
DIAL	CREAM
WINDING MECHANISM	MECHANICAL
CALIBRE	120
DIAMETER	38MM
MATERIAL	STEEL
STRAP	LEATHER
TYPE	SIMPLE

VULCAIN
CAL. 120

The chief innovation of this movement,
developed from 1947, lies in its two barrels:
one for adjusting the time, the other for the
alarm function.

INSPIRED BY NATURE

Vulcain was founded in 1858 by the
Ditisheim family in La Chaux-de-Fonds,
Switzerland. The company was renowned for
its pocket watches and, during the 1940s,
it specialized in wristwatches. At this time
Robert, a member of the third generation,
dreamed of making a model that was
robust, waterproof, elegant and equipped
with an alarm. This function, which was
first developed in the 16th century, already
existed on pocket watches (see page 14).
However, it was hard to miniaturize, and the
design was not at the point where it could be
incorporated in a wristwatch: its vibrations
were silent and altered the energy required
for accuracy. From 1942, Robert Ditisheim
and his engineers worked on this project
and asked the physicist Paul Langevin for
his advice. He came up with the example of
a cricket, which was capable of producing a
loud noise despite its slender body.

CALIBRE 120

From the start of the development work,
the teams at Vulcain made a prototype:
the calibre 120. This hand-wound
mechanism solved the vibration problem.
To do this, it used two barrels (see page 26):
one for rewinding the movement, the other
for the alarm function. Keeping the two
independent meant the alarm did not use
the movement's energy and vibrations could
resound for about 25 seconds. To address the
volume issue, they drew inspiration from
the membrane, which allows the cricket to
produce its sound. The company registered
a patent for a method to produce a sound
using a hammer that struck an internal
membrane. The latter was amplified by a

double case main plate that was waterproof
and perforated. After five years' research, the
Cricket was unveiled to the public in 1947. A
resounding commercial success, the following
year it won the International Chronometry
Competition at the Neuchâtel Observatory.

THE WATCH OF PRESIDENTS

This watch met with international success,
especially in the United States, where people
rushed to buy the first alarm wristwatch.
It became the official president's watch in
1953, when Harry Truman was given a
model, engraved with the words 'One more
please' on the back, by the White House
News Photographers Association. His
successor, Dwight Eisenhower, more often
associated with the Rolex Day-Date (see
page 50), also owned a Cricket. Richard
Nixon, then vice-president, was given his by
the National Association of Watch and Clock
Collectors in 1955. The model's greatest
fan was undoubtedly the 36th president,
Lyndon Johnson who, as well as owning
one, had the habit of giving Crickets to his
colleagues. During the 1960s, the watch was
so successful that Vulcain launched a dive
watch and versions for women. However,
the quartz crisis (see page 209) affected
the company, which refused to abandon
mechanical movements. In 1988, it was
suggested to Michael Ditisheim, Robert's
son, that he revive the tradition of giving
the watch to American presidents. Since
then Ronald Reagan, George H W Bush,
Gerald Ford, Jimmy Carter, Bill Clinton,
Barack Obama, Donald Trump and
Joe Biden have all been given theirs.

MEMOVOX

JAEGER-LECOULTRE – 1950

In 1950, Jaeger-LeCoultre followed in Vulcain's footsteps and launched a wristwatch with an alarm function. Six years later, the manufacturer developed the concept to make it automatic.

SEE OPPOSITE	**1970 MODEL**
MANUFACTURER	**JAEGER-LECOULTRE**
MODEL	**MEMOVOX SPEED BEAT**
REFERENCE	**N/A**
DIAL	**TWO-TONE: SILVER AND BLUE**
WINDING MECHANISM	**AUTOMATIC**
CALIBRE	**916**
DIAMETER	**37MM**
MATERIAL	**STEEL**
STRAP	**LEATHER**
TYPE	**SIMPLE**

**JAEGER-LECOULTRE
CAL. 916**

The automatic Bumper movement used for the calibre 825 was replaced by a free rotor: the calibre 916.

THE VOICE OF MEMORY

In 1950, Jaeger-LeCoultre followed Vulcain and its Cricket (see page 172) by creating the Memovox – 'voice of memory'. Driven by the hand-wound calibre 489, it featured two crowns so that the alarm and time could be adjusted separately. The company marketed the watch as a travelling companion that 'remembers, warns and wakes'. Thanks to its elegance and functionality, it quickly won over celebrities. One of these was a new Swiss resident, Charlie Chaplin. In 1953, the authorities in the canton of Vaud, home to the Jaeger-LeCoultre factory in the heart of the Joux valley, gave him a Memovox.

THE FIRST AUTOMATIC CALIBRE WITH AN ALARM FUNCTION

In order to acquire a new, sportier clientele, Jaeger-LeCoultre decided to make the first automatic watch with an alarm function. In 1956, just a few years after its initial launch, the Memovox was fitted with an automatic calibre, the 815, based on a Bumper movement (see page 58). Since it no longer needed rewinding, more and more lovers of outdoor pursuits bought it. In 1959, the manufacturer took the concept further, deciding to offer its new customers a dive watch: the Deep Sea. It was still equipped with the 815 and was the first waterproof watch to feature an alarm. Thanks to vibrations that were perceptible even underwater, divers could be warned about the length of their dive. That same year, the calibre 825 added a date function to the watch. The movement was also fitted to the company's second automatic dive watch with an alarm function, the Polaris, which had a 42mm case made by Piquerez

(see page 148). Despite everything, this first generation was fragile. In 1970, thanks to the calibre 916, Jaeger-LeCoultre was able to replace the Bumper movement with a free rotor. Frequency increased from 18,800 to 28,800 vibrations per hour, allowing new levels of accuracy to be attained. These movements were first fitted to the Speed Beat models, and then to the second-generation Polaris, which now featured a large case.

EVOLUTION

Although it developed mechanically, the elegant Memovox managed to retain its essential characteristics. In 1989, the manufacturer unveiled the first alarm calibre that also featured a perpetual calendar: the 919. In 2005, the Master Grand Réveil was given a double alarm device, which offered the choice of either a chime or a vibration mode, for a completely discreet alert. In 2007, the Master Compressor Extreme W-Alarm, featuring the calibre 912, gave the watch a universal time function, so the user could get their bearings in any time zone, as well as a digital display, which indicated the exact moment when the alarm would sound, in hours and minutes. Since 2008, the new versions of the Memovox have featured the 956 movement, its number contains a reference to the date when the first automatic calibre with alarm function was launched: 1956.

PERPETUAL CALENDAR

PATEK PHILIPPE – 1962

When the iconic Patek Philippe ref. 3448 appeared in 1962,
it was the first automatic wristwatch with a perpetual calendar.
The celebrities who contributed to its legendary status include Andy Warhol
and Ringo Starr, the drummer of the Beatles.

SEE OPPOSITE	1965 MODEL
MANUFACTURER	PATEK PHILIPPE
MODEL	PERPETUAL CALENDAR PADELLONE
REFERENCE	3448
DIAL	SILVER
WINDING MECHANISM	AUTOMATIC
CALIBRE	27-460 Q
DIAMETER	37.5MM
MATERIAL	YELLOW GOLD
STRAP	LEATHER
TYPE	SIMPLE

PATEK PHILIPPE
CAL. 27-460 Q

The calibre 27-460 followed the
12-600. Its name is a reference
to its dimensions: it is 27mm in
diameter and 4.60mm thick.

PERPETUAL CALENDERS

Perpetual calendars are watches that display
the date, day, month and often the moon
phase, automatically taking the length of
the months and leap years into account.
Patek Philippe has a long history of making
this mechanism, a true masterpiece of
craftsmanship and miniaturization. In 1925,
the Swiss company created the world's first
wristwatch featuring this function, using
a hand-wound movement that had been
designed in 1898 for a woman's pendant
watch. In 1937, it went on to fit a ref. 96
(see page 36) with a retrograde perpetual
calendar – this was quite a feat given the
limited production of that model. During the
1940s, the ref. 1526 became Patek Philippe's
first watch with a perpetual calendar to
go into regular production. This reference
established the style with its characteristic
dial configuration: two rectangular apertures
side by side for the day and month at
12 o'clock, and a subdial for the moon phase
and the date at 6 o'clock. This design became
the standard for the models created by Patek
Philippe. In 1962, the perpetual calendar
entered the automatic era with the ref. 3448.

THE FIRST AUTOMATIC
PERPETUAL CALENDAR

If the ref. 3448 is sought after today, it is
because of its calibre 27-460 Q. A descendant
of the 12-600 AT designed in 1953, it is
considered by many to be the most beautiful
automatic movement in the history of
watchmaking. In its time, it was the most
expensive ever made, and its name refers to
its chief characteristics: a diameter of 27mm

(12 lignes) and a thickness of 4.60mm. The
complication takes into account not only
months with 31, 30 and 28 days, but also
leap years. Moreover, the watch has a moon
phase display surrounded by a date wheel at
6 o'clock, and two apertures showing the day
and month at 12 o'clock – a Patek Philippe
signature feature. Used until the 1980s,
with the ref. 3450, this calibre was replaced
by the micro-rotor 240 Q, which allowed the
case to be thinner. This was an exceptionally
long time for a movement to remain in use.
The modern design of ref. 3448 was the work
of the case manufacturer Antoine Gerlach.
Named Padellone (Italian for 'big frying pan')
the watch features a harmonious 37.5mm
case and dauphine hands (see page 22), but
unlike its predecessors, the minute scale and
second hand are absent.

AN EXCEPTIONAL WATCH

It is said that a total of 586 of these
watches were made over 20 years, until the
introduction of ref. 3450, which featured a
leap year display. Although most models
were made in yellow gold, there were also
white gold variants and a few rare rose gold
ones. Only a collector who was close to the
Stern family had the privilege of having a
special platinum version made. Over time,
subtle differences appeared on the dial,
and some unique watches were made,
including a blue model.

TRI-COMPAX

UNIVERSAL GENÈVE – 1944

**The Tri-Compax was unveiled in Basel in 1944.
This watch brings together three complications: chronograph,
calendar and moon phase. It is part of the Compax collection,
which began in 1936, two years after the Compur.**

SEE OPPOSITE	1965 MODEL
MANUFACTURER	UNIVERSAL GENÈVE
MODEL	TRI-COMPAX
REFERENCE	222100-2
DIAL	SILVER
WINDING MECHANISM	MECHANICAL
CALIBRE	281
DIAMETER	36MM
MATERIAL	STEEL
STRAP	LEATHER
TYPE	SIMPLE

TRI-COMPAX

1934	COMPUR
1936	COMPAX
1944	TRI-COMPAX
1965	REF. 222100
1967	REF. 881101 ERIC CLAPTON

ORIGINS

The Universal Genève trademark was registered in 1894, when Numa Émile Descombes and Ulysse Georges Perret founded their company, Descombes et Perret. On Descombes' death in 1897, Perret joined forces with Louis Édouard Berthoud. Perret & Berthoud had a particularly strong presence in Italy and Spain, and also represented other brands, such as Zenith. In 1917, Universal Genève, which used movements made by other manufacturers, produced its first chronograph. Some chronographs were fitted with Lemania movements (see page 101), but most, including the watch launched in 1917, featured an example from another manufacturer, Martel Watch Co., which had been founded by Georges Pellaton-Steudler in 1911. Universal then specialized in complications, with some repeater watches and chronographs. During the 1930s, thanks to Raoul Perret, a Zenith director who became chairman of the board of Martel Watch Co., Universal chronographs conquered the world. The Tri-Compax was unveiled in Basel in 1944.

TRI-COMPAX FUNCTIONS

The Tri-Compax chronograph remained on sale until the end of the 1960s and was at the top of the Compax range. Its name refers to the three functions the watch offers: a calendar, a chronograph and a moon phase. It is generally driven by the calibre 281, invented in 1932. This column wheel movement is interesting because it was fitted to the first chronograph to offer the calendar complication. Developed in collaboration with Martel and shared with Zenith, it was produced for more than half a century. The Tri-Compax version, featuring a calendar and moon phase as well as the chronograph function, is the most representative of its type. Available in a variety of configurations over the years, the tool-watch-type steel models generally had luminous hands. The gold ones, which were more formal and elegant, featured blued steel hands instead. The steel versions from the 1960s are desirable: the ref. 881101/01, with its external bezel and Panda dial (see page 126), was owned by the guitarist Eric Clapton. Another, the ref. 222100, with a smooth bezel and internal scale, is also sought after. In order to make setting the calendar easier, these watches have a case with three discreet push-buttons on the left.

COMPAX, BI-COMPAX AND TRI-COMPAX

Thanks to the launch of the Compax model in 1936, then the Tri-Compax in 1944, Universal Genève was considered to be the greatest manufacturer of chronographs of its time. Although today the term Compax, which was invented by the company, refers to the number and arrangement of the subdials, it originally referred to the number of functions. Perhaps a watch with two subdials arranged horizontally at 3 o'clock (minutes) and 9 o'clock (hours) may be considered a Uni-Compax, but the name Bi-Compax is used. The term Compax refers to the chronographs with three counters arranged in a V, at 3, 6 and 9 o'clock (see page 84).

LUNE ASTRONOMIQUE

BREGUET – 1990s

For more than two centuries Breguet has lit up the world of
watchmaking with its complications and its distinctive features.
Engraved dials or hands make these watches immediately identifiable.

SEE OPPOSITE	2000 MODEL
MANUFACTURER	BREGUET
MODEL	LUNE ASTRONOMIQUE
REFERENCE	3040
DIAL	GOLD, ENGRAVED (CLOU DE PARIS)
WINDING MECHANISM	AUTOMATIC
CALIBRE	NO. 502 QS
DIAMETER	36MM
MATERIAL	GOLD
STRAP	LEATHER
TYPE	SIMPLE

DISTINCTIVE FEATURES

Whether in combination or not, these make a
Breguet immediately identifiable:

- ENGRAVED DIAL
- BREGUET HANDS
- FLUTING
- SECRET SIGNATURE
- BREGUET NUMERALS
- UNIQUE NUMBER
- WELDED LUGS

ABRAHAM-LOUIS BREGUET

Abraham-Louis Breguet made his reputation
and earned the respect of his contemporaries
in Paris thanks to his inventions. The most
famous of these was a tourbillon winding
and setting mechanism, patented in 1801.
He also developed a shock absorber, an
automatic rewinding system (perpetual
watch), a Breguet Phillips terminal curve
balance spring that allowed its beats to be
harmonized, as well as a tactile watch (that
allowed the user to tell the time by touch) in
1799. However, Breguet attached as much
importance to a watch's appearance as to
its inner workings. As watchmaker to the
court of Louis XVI, he counted several high-
ranking individuals among his customers,
including queen Marie Antoinette. During
his life Abraham-Louis Breguet was
designated a master watchmaker, appointed
watchmaker to the royal navy, and made
a member of France's academy of sciences
and a knight of the Légion d'honneur.

BREGUET SIGNATURE FEATURES

Thanks to the recognizable features of a
Breguet watch, it is the style that makes
the difference rather than a flagship model.
Since 1786, the dials have been engraved.
Identifiable by their *cloud de Paris*, grains
of barley (*grain d'orge*), chequerboard or
flinqué motifs (see page 22), they endow
each watch with a unique character.
Another signature feature is the hands,
which are offset by their tips that resemble
a hollow apple. Invented in 1783, the term
'Breguet hands' is used today. Similarly,
the calligraphy used for the indexes on some
dials is also known as 'Breguet'.

The cases have a distinctive style thanks
to their fluting – that is, the fine lines
around their edges. The unique character
of each watch was reinforced by giving it
a serial number. This tradition makes it
possible to keep track of a piece throughout
its lifetime. In 1795, to combat counterfeiting,
Breguet added a secret signature to his
dials. Therefore, although there are
many possible variations, a Breguet is
immediately identifiable.

LUNE ASTRONOMIQUE

A lunar month is roughly 29.5 days. During
that time, the moon goes through eight
phases, corresponding to the amount of light
it receives from the sun. Today, moon phase
watches show only four of these on their
dials: new moon, first quarter, full moon and
last quarter. On classic models the disc that
bears two moons is driven by a wheel with
59 teeth. A lunar month lasts exactly
29 days, 12 hours and 48 seconds – or 29.531
days. Over time, the display gets out of phase
with the real moon. In order to get around
this problem, top-of-the-range models, such
as the ref. 3040, feature a more complex
device named Lune Astronomique, which
comprises a wheel with 135 teeth. With
this system, the discrepancy between the
mechanism and the cycle of the moon is only
one day in every 122 years. Although above
all this function is a design feature, the ref.
3040 possesses another, more useful one:
the triple date (see page 168). The day and
the month are displayed in two apertures
at 12 o'clock, and the date by a serpentine
hand that points to an internal scale with
numbers to 31.

DUAL TIME

PATEK PHILIPPE – 1976

**Travel watches are part of Patek Philippe's history.
Midway between jewellery and watchmaking, the Dual Time,
a watch with a double time display, came out in the 1970s.**

SEE OPPOSITE	1976 MODEL
MANUFACTURER	PATEK PHILIPPE
MODEL	DUAL TIME GEMINI
REFERENCE	4404
DIAL	MALACHITE
WINDING SYSTEM	MECHANICAL
CALIBRE	13.5-320 × 2
DIAMETER	35 × 24MM
MATERIAL	WHITE GOLD
TYPE	MESH

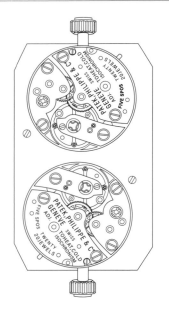

PATEK PHILIPPE
DUAL TIME

The manufacture of this watch combines
the work of highly skilled jewellers and
watchmakers. It is driven by two 13.5-320
calibres, the smallest Patek Philippe
movements.

PATEK PHILIPPE AND TRAVEL WATCHES

Travel watches have a special place in the
history of Patek Philippe. Since 1937, this
Swiss company has offered a World Time
model, fitted with a mechanism developed
by Louis Cottier, an independent Geneva
watchmaker. The basic calibres were
ébauches supplied by Patek Philippe, on
to which Cottier grafted a universal time
mechanism, which stands out thanks to two
special features: a synchronized 24-hour disc
that allows the time in different time zones
to be displayed; and time zones identified by
different cities in the world marked on the
bezel or a peripheral disc. Production of the
World Time was small, but it continued until
the watchmaker closed in 1966, before being
resumed in larger numbers, to the delight of
collectors, during the 2000s.

During the 1970s, a completely different
travel watch, midway between jewellery
and watchmaking, appeared. It was not
featured in the catalogue and was reserved
for privileged customers of the Geneva-based
company. A special configuration and unique
design make it possible to tell the time in two
time zones.

REF. 4404 DUAL TIME

Ref. 4404, named Gemini (as in twins), is
a watch with a double time display, made
by Patek Philippe in very small numbers
between 1976 and 1979. Eight of these
Dual Time watches have been identified,
and it is believed that fewer than 30 were
produced. Those that are known are in white
gold and fitted with a Milanese mesh strap
(see page 150) attached to a case that was

made in two forms: one with a full bezel and
another where the bezel has been replaced
by the strap attachment. The dimensions
of the watch (35 × 24mm) were selected to
appeal to both male and female customers.
The case was made by Ateliers Réunis in
Geneva and the strap by another Geneva
craftsman, Jean-Pierre Ecoffey. These
exceptional watches are driven by 13.5-320
calibres, the smallest movements created
and used by the company since 1959. The
dial of each one that has been identified to
date has unique features. Made by Cadrans
Stern Frères – a family business – they
are gold-plated and covered in precious or
semi-precious stones such as onyx, jade,
lapis lazuli, mother-of-pearl or malachite
(see page 53).

Considering their rarity, the literature
relating to these models is limited, very little
is known and mysteries remain. However,
what is certain is that this watch, with
its unique design, is at the intersection of
jewellery and watchmaking and the work of
highly skilled craftsmen.

MINUTE REPEATER

VACHERON CONSTANTIN – 1992

**Vacheron Constantin is one of the oldest watchmakers in the world.
Its motto is: 'Do the best possible, which is always possible.'
Since the 19th century, it has specialized in grand complications.**

SEE OPPOSITE	2000 MODEL
MANUFACTURER	VACHERON CONSTANTIN
MODEL	MINUTE REPEATER PERPETUAL CALENDAR
REFERENCE	30020
DIAL	SILVER, SIGMA
WINDING MECHANISM	MECHANICAL
CALIBRE	1755
DIAMETER	36MM
MATERIAL	PLATINUM
STRAP	LEATHER
TYPE	FOLDING BUCKLE

VACHERON CONSTANTIN

1731	BIRTH OF JEAN-MARC VACHERON
1755	FOUNDING OF VACHERON CONSTANTIN
1810	MINUTE REPEATER COMPLICATION IN A POCKET WATCH
1941	MINUTE REPEATER COMPLICATION IN A WRISTWATCH (CALIBRE 4261)
1992	INTRODUCTION OF CALIBRE 1755
2009	INTRODUCTION OF CALIBRE 1731

A VENERABLE WATCH MANUFACTURER

Vacheron Constantin is a Swiss watchmaking company whose history dates back to 1755. Jean-Marc Vacheron, son of a manual worker from Geneva, quickly attained the rank of master watchmaker. He worked in the manner of a *cabinotier* (independent watchmaker) – that is, in partnership with different specialist craftsmen who worked from home. Jean-Marc Vacheron left the responsibility of looking after the family business to his second child, Abraham. The latter picked up the torch and handed it on to his own son, Jacques-Barthélemy, who joined forces with François Constantin on 1 January 1819. The business continued to operate under the name Vacheron & Constantin. In 1839, Georges-Auguste Leschot, a mechanical genius, joined the company. The machinery he perfected made it possible to mass-produce components, contributing to the firm's ongoing success. The company's emblem, the Maltese cross, was inspired by the shape of a watch component and was first used in 1862.

A SPECIALIST IN GRAND COMPLICATIONS

In 1884, Vacheron Constantin was the first manufacturer to develop a precision perpetual calendar in a pocket watch. In 1901, it set up the Atelier des Grandes Complications (complications workshop). This produced a *savonnette* (or hunter) pocket watch in 18-carat red gold, which combined a minute repeater, single push-button chronograph with fly-back hand and perpetual calendar (see page 171).

The minute repeater was a Vacheron Constantin speciality – it first developed this complication in a pocket watch in 1810. The mechanism chimes to indicate the time and was invented in the 18th century so that the user of the watch could tell the time in the dark. Activating a push-button on the left causes and hammers to strike a series of gongs: a deep sound for the hours, a higher-pitched one for the minutes and alternating ones for the quarter-hours. This mechanical orchestra is one of the most technical complications. In 1941, Vacheron Constantin launched its first wristwatch featuring just one complication, the calibre 4261, which had a minute repeater fitted inside an ultra-thin movement.

PATRIMONY RANGE

With its 260 years of experience, Vacheron Constantin not only occupies a rightful place on the international scene, but above all possesses an expertise that won fame with its Patrimony range in 1992. With these watches, the company introduced an ultra-thin minute repeater: the calibre 1755 (a reference to the year the manufacturer was founded). This movement, developed by Dubois Dépraz, is based on the calibre 4261 of the 1940s. Only 200 were made, of which about 30 had a perpetual calendar. The ref. 30020 Patrimony, with teardrop-shaped platinum lugs, blends tradition with modernity as it is fitted with this minute repeater/perpetual calendar movement. Not many were made, and it was replaced by the calibre 1731, 0.62mm wider than the 1755 – this time, named after the year of its founder's birth.

MONO-RATTRAPANTE

BOVET – 1936

From the 1930s to the 1950s, Bovet produced excellent chronographs.
In 1936, the company registered a patent for a
mono-rattrapante chronograph system.

SEE OPPOSITE	1940 MODEL
MANUFACTURER	BOVET
MODEL	MONO-RATTRAPANTE
REFERENCE	N/A
DIAL	SILVER
WINDING MECHANISM	MECHANICAL
CALIBRE	VALJOUX 84
DIAMETER	34MM
MATERIAL	STEEL
STRAP	N/A
TYPE	N/A

VALJOUX
CAL. 84

Bovet specialized in fly-back and
mono-rattrapante complications.
Watches featuring the latter function were
designed using the Valjoux 84 as a base.

FROM FLEURIER TO CANTON

After being trained in watchmaking by his
father in Fleurier, Switzerland, Édouard
Bovet moved to London. In 1814, his two
brothers joined him there. In 1818, while
he was working for the Maniac company,
he was sent to Guangzhou, China, to repair
watches. Four years later, Édouard decided
to set up his own business, assisted by his
two brothers, who had remained in London,
and their father in Fleurier. The company
made finely finished pocket watches with
enamelled dials, transparent backs and so
forth but without grand complications. It
was the first to offer Chinese characters on
its dials. Such was its success that the term
'povay' – Bovet pronounced with a Chinese
accent – became synonymous with watches
in that country. On Édouard's death in
1848, his heirs, who had little interest in
watchmaking, sold the company. The Bovet
family – through Jean and Albert, who were
also watchmakers – bought it back in the
1930s. In 1948, Favre-Leuba bought the
brand and its factory and produced Bovet
watches until 1950, thereafter using the
company to make its own watches until 1966.

MONO-RATTRAPANTE

In 1936, Bovet registered a patent for a
mono-rattrapante chronograph system. In
a normal fly-back watch, two superimposed
hands run when the chronograph is started.
In order to measure intermediate times, the
watch allows the user to stop just one hand
while the other continues on its course. Most
often with a mono-rattrapante, the push-
button at 2 o'clock acts as a one-push-button,
allowing the chronograph to be started,
stopped and returned to zero. Some of the
company's watches offer a second crown
on the push-button at 2 o'clock, allowing
it, once stopped, to resume running. When
pressed firmly, the push-button at 4 o'clock
stops the chronograph's hand; releasing the
push-button causes the hand to move to the
position where it would have been if it had
not been stopped. Bovet's watches featuring
this complication were designed using the
Valjoux 84 as a base; at the time Bovet
shared a contract of exclusivity with the
firm. Bovet chronographs from that date can
be recognized by their lacquered (gilt) or two-
tone silver dials. Although a very few models
have unusually shaped cases, some of those
made by Spillman have a sporty shape.

RESURRECTION

Bovet returned to Fleurier in 1989, following
its acquisition by Michel Parmigiani, who
in turn sold the company in 1997. In 2001,
Bovet was bought by Pascal Raffy, who
has concentrated on making exceptional
watches. In 2007, he bought the Bovet
family's château in the village of Môtiers. In
2013, the brand was renamed Bovet 1822,
in homage to the date that it was founded.
That same year, Pascal Raffy committed to
making fewer than 2,000 watches per year,
and devoting 20 per cent of the company's
production to unique pieces. In November
2018 a Bovet 1822 won the Aiguille d'or, the
most distinguished award at the Grand Prix
d'Horlogerie in Geneva.

SPORTS
WATCHES

CHAPTER 5

GÉRALD GENTA
THE PICASSO OF WATCHES

FACT SHEET N°14

Described as 'the Fabergé of watches' by the auction house Christie's,
and by collectors as 'the Picasso of watches', this Geneva artist and watchmaker
created and designed models for the biggest names in the modern watch industry.

STARTING OUT AT UNIVERSAL GENÈVE, THEN ON TO OMEGA

Born in Geneva in 1931 to a Swiss mother and Italian father, Gérald Genta obtained his Swiss federal diploma as a jeweller and goldsmith in 1951. Three years later he was employed by the Universal Genève company. In the 1950s he created the Polerouter model for them (see page 64). In the mid-1960s he designed two more models that would go down in history: the Golden Shadow and the White Shadow, both of which contained an extra-flat micro-rotor. Thanks to these creations his talent was noticed, and Omega asked him to refresh the Constellation, which had been created in 1952 (see page 60).

He was involved in the development of several designs, working on indexes, dials and cases. At least two models are attributed to him: the ref. 14900 Pie Pan, with onyx indexes, and the barrel-shaped ref. 168.009, known as the C-Shape. In 1968, Patek Philippe, impressed by Universal Genève's Shadow range, hired Genta and he contributed to the design of the Golden Ellipse (see page 38).

THE 1970s – THE PEAK OF HIS CAREER

In 1968, flush with his early successes, Genta started his own company using his surname, in 1969. An inventor and artist of genius, he divided his time between his own enterprise and other assignments. In 1972, he shook up the standards of traditional watchmaking forever with the creation of the Royal Oak for Audemars Piguet. Its integrated strap was designed in a single night and based on a childhood memory of a deep-sea diver (see page 192). With this watch Genta invented the concept of sporty chic. In 1976, he worked for Patek Philippe again. The story goes that he sketched the design for the Nautilus, this time inspired by a porthole, in five minutes (see page 194). That same year, IWC called on his services to modernize its Ingenieur model and create some watches for its new luxury sports range, Club SL (see page 196). During these years, Genta worked with the Italian company Bulgari on the launch of the Bulgari Bulgari model, a watch inspired by ancient Rome and with a bezel engraved with the company's name in two places.

GENTA'S LEGACY

Thanks to his reputation, this designer-watchmaker could do whatever he wanted. In the 1980s, he obtained a special licence from the US Walt Disney company, authorizing him to launch an edition of his watches decorated with its characters, as Ingersoll had done in the past (see page 30). In the process he invented a new way of telling the time using retrograde and bi-retrograde movements. In 1999, the Genta brand was bought by Bulgari. Genta later founded the Gerald Charles watch brand in 2000, which still exists independent of Bulgari.

Since 2010, Genta watches have existed only under this label. Gérald Genta died in 2011, but his legacy and memory were kept alive by his wife, Évelyne. In 2019, she founded the Gérald Genta Heritage Association, which encourages young talented individuals to perfect their art. The association has set up an annual Gérald Genta prize, aimed at rewarding 'talented young designers and those with great potential in the sector of the high art of watchmaking'.

JÖRG HYSEK
A REBEL DESIGNER

FACT SHEET N°15

The much-missed Gérald Genta was unquestionably the most renowned designer in contemporary watchmaking, to the extent that many attribute to him the design of the Vacheron Constantin 222 – however, it was actually the work of another talented designer: Jörg Hysek.

222 – THE MASTERPIECE

Born in Berlin in 1953, Jörg Hysek arrived in Geneva with his parents in 1960, just before the Berlin Wall was built. After two years studying micromechanics in Bienne, he enrolled at the professional watchmaker's school in Pforzheim. In 1973, his passion for sculpture led him to study at the Royal Academy of Arts in London. Once his training was completed, Hysek returned to Switzerland to work in the watchmaking industry. He spent four years at Rolex before setting up his own design company, Hysek Styling. His first client, Vacheron Constantin, asked him to create a sporty chic watch in keeping with the fashions of the time. Aged just 24, Hysek oversaw the design of Projet 222, which resulted in the creation of the Swiss company's flagship model (see page 198). With Vacheron Constantin he won prestigious awards, including the Grand Prix de la Ville de Genève, in 1984, for a watch with an adjustable strap.

OTHER CREATIONS BY THE DESIGNER

Although Breguet was accustomed to making elegant watches with grand complications, in 1990 it called upon Hysek's studio to create a sporty watch: the Marine (French for 'navy'). In 1815, Abraham-Louis Breguet was made official supplier to the French navy; inspired by this military heritage, Hysek revisited Breguet's design features (see page 180) and reinvented them in a modern watch. The Breguet Marine had two distinctive features: an oversized crown and a crown guard to protect it (a first for the brand). The sporty Marine range is still in the catalogue. In 1997, Hysek created the Kirium model for TAG Heuer, a modern take on the TAG Heuer 4000 series. More elegant and versatile than the original, the watch had an integrated strap and was designed as a coherent whole. It remained in production until 2008, and the model was successfully produced in numerous versions. Also in the 1990s, Tiffany & Co. launched the Streamerica line, a homage to the aesthetic of 1930s American industrial design. It comprised jewellery, pocket knives and keyrings, but also watches. The mastermind behind it was none other than Jörg Hysek.

AN INDEPENDENT, MAVERICK WATCHMAKER

Over time, more big brands such as Boucheron, Cartier, Ebel and Seiko used the services of Hysek's studio. In parallel, when the designer launched his eponymous brand in 1999, it included high-end pens. He discontinued it some time later, but was involved in the creation of sophisticated modern models such as the HD3 Complication. Always uncompromising in both his technical and design choices – if sometimes (too) bold – this designer with a rebellious spirit was a major actor in the watchmaking sector. Hysek followed only one principle: 'A good designer must always be ahead of their time.' Although with hindsight the success of the 222 model proved him right, for the rest, time will tell.

ROYAL OAK

AUDEMARS PIGUET – 1972

**Designed in 1970 by Gérald Genta, developed in 1971
and launched in 1972, Audemars Piguet's Royal Oak established
a new style: sporty chic. It was the start of a collection.**

SEE OPPOSITE	**1973 MODEL**
MANUFACTURER	**AUDEMARS PIGUET**
MODEL	**ROYAL OAK**
REFERENCE	**5402**
DIAL	**BLUE 'TAPISSERIE'**
WINDING MECHANISM	**AUTOMATIC**
CALIBRE	**2121**
DIAMETER	**39MM**
MATERIAL	**STEEL**
STRAP	**STEEL**
TYPE	**INTEGRATED**

A NON-EXISTENT WATCH

Audemars Piguet was founded in 1875 in Le Brassus, Switzerland, by Jules-Louis Audemars and Edward-Auguste Piguet. From 1882 onwards, the company produced watches with complications. In 1970, it attained the highest excellence in watchmaking. Despite this, like other manufacturers, Audemars Piguet was affected by the quartz crisis (see page 209). To relaunch itself, it put its faith in the Basel trade fair. The day before, the company's boss, Georges Golay, met with the Italian agent Carlo De Marchi, the Swiss Charles Bauty and the Frenchman Charles Dorot. These three set Golay the challenge of designing a mass-produced steel watch that was suitable for modern life by being both sporty and elegant. Against all expectations Golay accepted the challenge. He worked in partnership with the independent designer Gérald Genta to ensure that he could achieve the impossible.

FEATURES AND NAME

On the night of 10 April, Genta drew inspiration from a childhood memory of a diver to create his design: an ultra-thin octagonal watch, with visible, hexagonal screws, an engraved dial and an integrated strap. He was entrusted with seeing the project through to its completion. For the case, he went to Favre & Perret, a specialist in gold cases. Since steel is extremely difficult to work, the prototypes were made in grey gold. However, an order was placed for 1,000 steel cases. For the dial he turned to the Stern brothers (see page 36) and opted for a midnight blue tapestry motif. The thinnest automatic movement with date

function available at the time was chosen: the calibre 2121, created by LeCoultre & Cie and Vacheron Constantin. The integrated strap was entrusted to the craftsmen at Gay Frères (see page 150). Despite their experience, they did not succeed in attaining the level of specification demanded. Like the cases, the straps were reworked by the watchmakers in Le Brassus. A year later, in April 1971 in Basel, Golay presented the grey gold prototype to the three men who had set him the challenge. De Marchi and Bauty committed to buying 400 each. What was still missing was a name. Safari and Excalibur were mentioned, but De Marchi made a suggestion that struck a chord: Royal Oak. The name paid homage to the warships of the Royal Navy, with their metal armour. It also evoked the species of tree in which King Charles I of England supposedly took refuge. On 6 December 1971, Audemars Piguet registered its patent and Gérald Genta was named as the inventor.

1972 – OFFICIAL LAUNCH

The launch was planned for 1972 in Basel, but the final months before it were tense. Gérald Genta had left, and within the company there were doubts about the design. The cost of production meant that the ref. 5402 was priced at £345 (3,300 Swiss francs), three times the price of a Submariner. At the time, it was the most expensive steel watch on the market. At its launch it was modestly successful, but in 1974, Gianni Agnelli wore one in public and orders multiplied. The Series A, limited to 1,000 units, eventually increased to 2,000. In 1975, Series B appeared, followed by C and finally, in 1978, Series D. More than 6,000 were sold in total.

NAUTILUS

PATEK PHILIPPE – 1976

In 1976, Patek Philippe followed Audemars Piguet into the sporty chic market with the Nautilus. It too called on the designer Gérald Genta to create this watch featuring legendary curves.

SEE OPPOSITE	2006 MODEL
MANUFACTURER	PATEK PHILIPPE
MODEL	NAUTILUS JUMBO
REFERENCE	5711
DIAL	BLUE LIGNES
WINDING MECHANISM	AUTOMATIC
CALIBRE	324 SC
DIAMETER	43MM
MATERIAL	STEEL
STRAP	STEEL
TYPE	INTEGRATED

A RECORD ANNIVERSARY

At the end of 2021, Patek Philippe made 5711 with a sky-blue dial, limited to 170 watches, to celebrate the 170th anniversary of its collaboration with Tiffany & Co. The first of these was sold a few days later for the record price of £5 million ($6.5 million).

A SKETCH IN FIVE MINUTES

When Patek Philippe introduced the Nautilus, it was not the first company to make this type of steel watch. The first of its kind had been made by its direct competitor Audemars Piguet (see page 192). Like the other Swiss manufacturers, Patek Philippe was affected by the quartz crisis (see page 209) and, like Audemars Piguet, it called on the designer Gérald Genta to help it. He claimed it took him just five minutes to design the watch. Knowing that the Stern family loved sailing, Genta drew his inspiration from portholes and designed the Nautilus in a flash. The sketch was reminiscent of the Royal Oak: the two watches share an octagonal shape and an integrated strap. But the curves of the Nautilus, with its 'ears' on either side, are softer, more anatomical and less sporty.

ONE OF THE MOST EXPENSIVE WATCHES

Since Patek Philippe was accustomed to gold and complications, mere steel was not enough. The manufacturer made it known that this was the most expensive steel watch ever produced. Indeed, each component was the subject of special work. Genta supplied Jean-Pierre Frattini with the technical plans for making a case waterproof to 120m: a single block of steel where the calibre was inserted from the dial side and closed like a porthole thanks to a second part, consisting of the bezel, the glass and the 'ears'. Although Gay Frères made the first straps, the overall manufacture of the watch was entrusted to Les Ateliers Réunis. Like the Royal Oak, the watch was driven by the calibre 28-255 C, based on the 920, developed by LeCoultre & Cie and Vacheron Constantin. The engraved dial also recalled the Audemars Piguet, but this time it was grey with a blue sheen and horizontal grooves. The watch's name, Nautilus, was inspired by that of the submarine in Jules Verne's novel *Twenty Thousand Leagues under the Sea*. The ref. 3700, introduced in 1976, was quickly nicknamed Jumbo on account of its size (42mm). Despite its diameter, at 7.60mm it was still thin.

LEGACY

At its launch, the ref. 3700 got a lukewarm reception. Success came during the 1980s, thanks to two models of more modest dimensions, the ref. 4700 and 3800. In 1998, a power reserve complication was added in addition to the date and a black dial without grooves was introduced. In 2005, the ref. 3712, a variant with a triple complication, was launched. A year later the model celebrated its 30th anniversary. Several variants were unveiled, but it was the ref. 5711, an evolution of the original design, which was an immediate hit. It had a calibre that was made in-house, a dial with a pronounced blue sheen and a central second hand. Unlike the old monobloc version, the bezel was fixed on a case that was 1mm wider and made up of three parts. Such was the enthusiasm for this watch that Patek Philippe could not meet demand. In January 2021, the manufacturer announced its decision to discontinue its steel reference. It was replaced by the ref. 5811 in white gold a few months later.

GOLF CLUB SL

IWC – 1976

In 1976, IWC asked Gérald Genta to redesign its Ingenieur model, which had
been launched in 1955. That same year, the Club SL range was unveiled.
Although documentation about it is lacking, the design of some
models is reminiscent of Genta's style.

SEE OPPOSITE	1976 MODEL
MANUFACTURER	IWC
MODEL	GOLF CLUB SL
REFERENCE	1830
DIAL	BLACK
WINDING MECHANISM	AUTOMATIC
CALIBRE	8541
DIAMETER	34MM
MATERIAL	STEEL
STRAP	STEEL
TYPE	INTEGRATED

IWC INGENIEUR SL
REF. 1832

The watch has similar characteristics to
Genta's first creation, the Royal Oak. Thanks
to its antimagnetic properties it is thicker,
plus it has visible screws and a strap
that is integrated with the case.

INTERNATIONAL WATCH CO.

Florentine Ariosto Jones was born in 1841
in the United States. He was determined to
produce Swiss-quality movements for the
American market and crossed the Atlantic to
Switzerland. On his arrival in Schaffhausen
in 1868, he met Heinrich Moser, who made
wristwatches for Russian tsars. Together
they founded the International Watch
Company. Although his dream of conquest
collapsed with the introduction of new
customs duties in the United States, Jones
nevertheless succeeded in making IWC a
name to be reckoned with. In 1879, after
going bankrupt twice, the company was
taken over by the Rauschenbach machine
manufacturer. In 1885, it produced the first
pocket watches with a digital display. During
the 1930s two Portuguese businessmen
made a surprising request: they wanted to
develop a steel wristwatch with a movement
capable of rivalling the accuracy of a marine
chronometer. The company installed a
pocket watch movement in a wristwatch,
and thus the Portuguese IWC was born.
At the same time, the company designed
watches for pilots, including the antimagnetic ref. IW436.

INGENIEUR

Twenty years later, IWC perfected antimagnetic protection and created a new
watch aimed specifically at professionals:
the Ingenieur. Like the Milgauss (see page
160) it had a mild steel cage. The ref. 666,
unveiled in 1955 and developed by Albert
Pellaton, who was IWC's technical director at
the time, had the first automatic movement
with bidirectional winding. In this system,
winding was accomplished in both of the
rotor's directions of movement. For some
20 years, the highly technical Ingenieur
featured a classic design. With the quartz
crisis looming (see page 209), IWC decided
to call on Genta, who had just got himself
noticed with the Royal Oak (see page
192). He designed a steel watch with an
integrated strap, whose shape resembled
that of a barrel. As in the Royal Oak, the
screws used to open the watch on the dial
side were visible. However, the Ingenieur
was not intended to be elegant as it was
a professional instrument. The 1976 ref.
1832, based on Genta's design, was wide
(40mm) but above all thick (14mm), given
the presence of the cage that contained
the automatic 8541 Pellaton. Although the
watch was not an outright success, technical
developments made it possible to refine the
model, which was consequently offered in
different variants.

CLUB SL SERIES

In 1967, IWC unveiled its dive watch: the
Aquatimer. Alongside it, the company
launched a leisure watch, the Yacht Club.
IWC aimed to offer a model that was both
sporty and classic. In 1976, hot on the heels
of the Ingenieur, IWC completely redesigned
the Yacht Club, in order to incorporate it into
a new range, Club SL, which comprised three
models: the Yacht Club II, the Polo Club SL
and the Golf Club SL. The SL could stand
for 'Sport Line' or 'Steel Line'. Production
continued until 1980; it is not known how
many watches were made.

222

VACHERON CONSTANTIN – 1977

Vacheron Constantin has a reputation for making luxurious, complicated watches. It celebrated its 222nd anniversary in 1977, with the launch of the 222 model.

SEE OPPOSITE	1978 MODEL
MANUFACTURER	VACHERON CONSTANTIN
MODEL	222 JUMBO
REFERENCE	44018
DIAL	GREY
WINDING MECHANISM	AUTOMATIC
CALIBRE	VC1121
DIAMETER	37MM
MATERIAL	STEEL
STRAP	STEEL
TYPE	INTEGRATED

A NEW STYLE

During the 1960s there were two kinds of watch: sporty and/or professional, and elegant. The following decade saw a revolution in style that produced a new kind that was initiated by Audemars Piguet and Gérald Genta (see page 192): the sporty chic watch. In 1975, faced with ever stiffer competition from quartz (see page 209), Vacheron Constantin, which was accustomed to making luxury, complicated watches, entered this new sector with the Chronomètre Royal, ref. 42001. Thanks to its octagonal case and bezel, this first steel watch with an integrated strap opened up new design possibilities. It was made for two years then disappeared from the catalogue. That same year, in Basel, Vacheron Constantin unveiled its novelty: the 222, a watch created by a young designer named Jörg Hysek (see page 191), then aged 24, who had just left Rolex in order to work independently.

222ND ANNIVERSARY

The watch was named 222 because it was launched on the manufacturer's 222nd anniversary. Hysek designed a steel watch that displayed the famous Maltese cross in the right-hand corner of its case at 5 o'clock, and featured an engraved bezel and an integrated strap – the work of the craftsmen at Gay Frères (see page 150). The model was sold in three sizes: 37mm and 34mm for the men's versions, and 24mm for a quartz women's version. The 222 was available in steel, gold and steel or all gold, with or without diamonds. The 37mm model, ref. 44018, was quickly nicknamed Jumbo by collectors.

It had a monobloc case waterproof to 120m with an antimagnetic cage (see page 159). Like the Royal Oak and the Nautilus, it featured a movement based on the automatic calibre 920, developed in collaboration with LeCoultre & Cie, which referred to it as VC1121. It was made for about eight years, and production is estimated at 3,000 units: 1,300 in 24mm size, 1,000 in 34mm and 700 in 37mm. The Jumbo models are especially rare. Although the dials of these models, originally grey-blue or anthracite grey in colour, were not engraved, today they have a subtle patina thanks to the passage of time (see page 102). The 222 was made until 1985, and was replaced by the Phidias at the end of the 1980s.

OVERSEAS RANGE AND REISSUE OF THE 222

The Vacheron Constantin Phidias was the inspiration for the Overseas, launched in 1996. This range, which has a travel theme, is still in production. It has evolved thanks to technical innovation and, as a result, numerous versions have appeared. Although it is still Vacheron Constantin's sporty chic watch, the company reissued the iconic 222 in 2022 for its Les Historiques collection. The watch featured the original characteristics of the ref. 44018 in gold. However, in keeping with the character of the collection, it is a modern reinterpretation that respects the 222's principles while benefiting from the latest advances.

QUARTZ
WATCHES

CHAPTER 6

ACCUTRON

BULOVA – 1960

As early as the 1950s, before quartz watches even appeared, Bulova was working on the tuning fork, a technology designed to improve autonomy and accuracy, which were weak points in the mechanical watches of the time. Although the quartz crisis caused it to fall out of use, Bulova continued to benefit from the success of its Accutron model.

SEE OPPOSITE	1970 MODEL
MANUFACTURER	BULOVA
MODEL	SPACEVIEW
REFERENCE	C 47549 STEEL
DIAL	N/A
WINDING MECHANISM	TUNING FORK
CALIBRE	214
DIAMETER	34MM
MATERIAL	STEEL
STRAP	LEATHER
TYPE	SIMPLE

BULOVA
TUNING FORK

The movement featured a U-shaped oscillator with two arms mounted with quartz crystals.

HISTORIC INNOVATIONS

Joseph Bulova, a Czech immigrant who had arrived in New York at the age of 19, founded Bulova in 1875. He was soon renowned for the aesthetic and technical qualities of his watches. In 1912, he opened a production facility in Bienne, Switzerland, and eight years later the company installed an observatory on the roof of a skyscraper so that it could make accurate measurements to ascertain universal time. In 1928, it unveiled its first radio alarm clock. Bulova was also a pioneer in the field of communications. It was the first company to broadcast a commercial on the radio in 1923, with the slogan: 'It's 8 AM, Bulova time', and on television in 1941.

ACCURACY THROUGH ELECTRONICS

Accutron stands for 'accuracy through electronics'. It was the first functioning electronic watch that used a tuning fork – a fork-shaped component used, until then, by musicians. The first mechanical clock using this mechanism was the work of Louis F. Breguet, grandson of the famous Abraham-Louis Breguet, in 1856. In 1952, the Elgin Watch Company launched the first electric watch: the Grade 725 – a mechanical watch powered by a battery. Although this way of powering a watch created a spectacular increase in autonomy, it did not improve accuracy at all. Bulova decided to do something about this, putting Max Hetzel, a Swiss engineer, in charge of the Accutron programme, with the aim of designing an electronic watch that was more accurate than a mechanical one.

Hetzel believed that adding a transistor would make the watch more accurate. He therefore replaced the balance with a tuning fork: a piece of metal with two parallel arms, welded together in a U shape and attached to a shaft. It was placed between two transistors and vibrated at 360 Hz, a higher frequency than a normal balance. A patent was registered in 1953, and the first prototype was operational in 1954. It attained an unmatched level of accuracy by losing only one minute per month.

A SHORT-LIVED SUCCESS

The Accutron was officially unveiled in 1960 by Bulova's CEO and went on sale in 1961. The first models were named Spaceview because the lack of a dial revealed the details of the movement. The Accutron was made available in several versions, but the Spaceview was the most popular. Thanks to this revolutionary technology, Bulova worked with NASA: although the Omega Speedmaster was the wristwatch chosen to go into space (see page 98), the company supplied on-board clocks for 46 space missions. An Accutron seismograph is still on the moon in a vehicle abandoned by the crew of Apollo 11. Production ended in 1977 with the quartz crisis (see page 209).

VENTURA

HAMILTON – 1957

On 3 January 1957 the American Hamilton Watch Company revolutionized watchmaking when it unveiled the first ever electric watch: the Ventura.

SEE OPPOSITE	2000 MODEL
MANUFACTURER	HAMILTON
MODEL	VENTURA
REFERENCE	H24411732
DIAL	BLACK
WINDING MECHANISM	QUARTZ
CALIBRE	F05.111
DIAMETER	32.3 × 50.3MM
MATERIAL	STEEL
STRAP	LEATHER
TYPE	SIMPLE

QUALITY AND ACCURACY

The Hamilton Watch Company (now Hamilton International Ltd.) was founded in Pennsylvania, United States, in 1892. From the outset, quality and accuracy were the company's two watchwords. Before World War I, the firm specialized in wristwatches that were supplied to pilots. In 1942, it stopped manufacturing for the wider public in order to supply watches to the armed forces again. In 1966, the company bought the Büren Watch Company. With Breitling, Heuer-Leonidas and Dubois Dépraz, it worked on a project for one of the first automatic chronograph movements (see page 94). Some 10 years earlier, in 1957, Hamilton had already revolutionized the industry by making the world's first electric watch powered by a miniature battery: the Ventura. Created by the industrial designer Richard Arbib, its futuristic looks – it was shaped like a shield – were an immediate sensation.

PROJECT X

With the Ventura, the energy needed for the movement to function was no longer supplied by manual winding via a crown or automatic winding by an oscillating weight, but by a small, button-shaped battery. This system, which marked the start of a new era, was the fruit of more than 10 years of research, which had begun in 1946 on the initiative of George Luckey, head of research and development at Hamilton. Under the code name Project X, two prototypes were designed between 1946 and 1952. All their components were manufactured in-house, with the exception of the cases. One of the chief difficulties in developing an electric calibre was finding a battery suitable for powering the movement. The solution was found thanks to the help of the National Carbon Company (now Energizer), which developed a special battery. While the Ventura was different technically, its unique triangular case singled it out for aesthetic reasons too.

THE WATCH OF THE FUTURE

The Ventura was unveiled in New York on 3 January 1957, in front of more than 120 international journalists. The 'watch of the future' was considered the most important innovation in watchmaking for several centuries and generated hundreds of articles in the press. Sadly, Hamilton had to deal with numerous customers returning their watches for after-sales service. The tendency of mass-produced H500 movements to break down was rectified in 1961 with the calibre H505. Despite this, the Ventura was a real commercial success: more than 11,500 were sold between 1957 and 1963. At the time it embodied American style thanks to Elvis Presley, who wore it in the movie *Blue Hawaii*. The year 1969 rang the death knell for electric mechanical watches when the first watch that made use of a quartz oscillator – the Seiko Astron – was unveiled. In 1970, Hamilton hit back by launching the Pulsar, 'which made the electric watch obsolete as well as the recently announced electro-mechanical quartz watch', according to the press release published in the *New York Times* on 10 May 1970. Despite everything, the Ventura, which can be spotted in the movie *Men in Black*, is still available in the catalogue in a quartz version.

ELECTRIC

TIMEX – 1961

**Timex is an American company known all over the world,
and its origins date back to 1857. It specializes
in affordable watches.**

SEE OPPOSITE	1969 MODEL
MANUFACTURER	TIMEX
MODEL	ELECTRIC
REFERENCE	N/A
DIAL	BLACK
WINDING MECHANISM	ELECTRIC
CALIBRE	84 LACO
DIAMETER	34MM
MATERIAL	CHROME
STRAP	LEATHER
TYPE	SIMPLE

WATERBURY CLOCK COMPANY

Timex's roots lie in the Waterbury Clock Company (WCC), which was founded in 1857. Until the end of the 19th century, this American concern, based in Connecticut's Naugatuck River valley – an area known as the Switzerland of America – made more than 20,000 watches a day. Supplying its main client, Ingersoll, allowed it to employ hundreds of staff and it became the world's biggest watch factory. However, WCC went bankrupt and was bought by Ingersoll, which took over Waterbury's factory and used it to make its watches. Several successes – a large pocket watch, the Jumbo, the $1 Yankee watch and, of course, the Mickey Mouse watch (see page 30) – brought about the revitalization of the company. During the 1940s, WCC was bought by Thomas Olsen and Joakim Lehmkuhl, two Norwegian industrialists who had fled the country as a result of World War II. Determined to support the war effort, they directed part of their production to the armed forces and were acknowledged by the US government, which bestowed the Army-Navy 'E' Award on the company, which was renamed United States Time Corporation for the occasion.

TIMEX CORPORATION

After the war, although the company continued its military production until the 1950s, it reoriented itself towards selling entry-level watches. It developed a new movement in which it replaced jewels (especially rubies) with a cheap metal alloy: armalloy. To showcase this technological advance, the company was renamed Timex (echoing SpaceX). Ten years later, half the watches sold in the United States were made by Timex, and in 1967 the company was the world's biggest watch manufacturer. The brand's provocative marketing campaigns were as famous as its watches. Timex relied on these to sell its watches directly to its customers, without a middleman. This enabled it to make a margin of only 30 per cent, at a time when retailers demanded 50 per cent. Also, its distribution strategy, which involved selling watches in unusual places – such as through newspaper advertisements, tobacconists and supermarkets – allowed Timex to attain prices never seen before.

ELECTRIC WATCHES

At the end of 1958, having previously tried to buy Bulova, Junghans and Gruen, Timex bought the German company Laco-Durowe. Laco had just developed a prototype electric watch, which had not yet gone into production, and as a result of this acquisition Timex became an important manufacturer in the electric watches segment. It was not until three years later that the first Timex Electric was officially unveiled. Some models were marked 'West Germany' on account of the origin of their movement. Electric watches were a major step forward for the company, but it later switched to quartz watches. A few years ago, Timex began to make mechanical watches; they are still sold at affordable prices.

CASIO 'BLUE THUNDER'
REF. AA-85 (MODULE 103)

Launched in 1981 and made famous by the 1983 action movie *Blue Thunder*,
this digital display model, worn by Roy Scheider,
features a quartz movement and is probably the rarest of its kind.

THE QUARTZ CRISIS

FACT SHEET N°16

During the 1970s the watchmaking industry experienced a technological breaking point with the adoption of the quartz oscillator from Japan. It caused a drastic fall in exports of Swiss watches. This was the quartz crisis.

BEFORE QUARTZ WATCHES

During the 1950s, long before the arrival of quartz watches, the American Bulova company was working on a technology that made it possible to increase the autonomy and accuracy of watches at its watch-component factory in Bienne, Switzerland. Max Hetzel took charge of the Accutron programme and replaced the balance with a tuning fork, a piece of metal with two parallel arms, welded together in a U shape and attached to a shaft. It was placed between two transistors and vibrated at 360 Hz, a higher frequency than a normal balance. The watch attained an unmatched level of accuracy of losing a minute per month (see page 202). In the United States, Hamilton revolutionized the industry by making the world's first electric watch, the Ventura (see page 204), which was driven by a miniature battery. These two systems marked the start of a new era and drove the Japanese company Seiko and the Swiss, who came together at the Centre Électronique Horloger (CEH), to follow this trend (see page 220).

HOW A QUARTZ WATCH WORKS

A quartz watch functions on electronic or electromechanical principles, and is generally powered by a battery. It uses an oscillator controlled by a quartz crystal resonator. A circuit causes the quartz crystals to vibrate and they indicate the watch's rate of oscillation. In a mechanical watch, the balance performs this function.

The oscillations of quartz are uniform and vibrate at a frequency of 32,768 Hz, which is significantly higher than mechanical watches. This frequency explains the accuracy of a quartz watch, which loses only about 0.5 seconds per day, whereas a mechanical watch may lose up to 30 seconds.

THE FIRST QUARTZ WATCH

In order to compete with the Swiss, Seiko devoted the 1950s to the search for accuracy. At the beginning of the 1960s, once the company had managed to establish itself, its management decided to focus the company's resources on a new technology: quartz. For Christmas 1969, after 10 years of development, the first ever quartz watch went on sale. It was called Astron. Boasting an accuracy of losing only 5 seconds per month and able to run continuously for a whole year, the watch was 100 times more accurate and had 250 times as much autonomy than any mechanical watch. At the same time, in 1970, the first Swiss quartz oscillator was launched with the Beta 21. However, the public gave the mechanism an unenthusiastic reception.

CRISIS

While Japanese and American companies continued to develop quartz watches and gain market share, in Switzerland there were many bankruptcies. Texas Instruments mass-produced watches at affordable prices, and in 1974 Casio began to make quartz watches with a digital display (see pages 208 and 224).

Between 1970 and 1983, the number of active Swiss watchmaking companies fell from 1,600 to 600, and the number of employees from 90,000 to just 28,000.

RESURGENCE

The industry was reborn thanks to Ernst Thomke and Nicolas G. Hayek. The former was put in charge of bringing together suppliers within a new company, ETA SA. He developed the Délirium, an ultra-thin quartz watch. He wanted to use his know-how to design an inexpensive watch that could be produced quickly. Lacking funds, he took his idea to Nicolas Hayek, who raised some finance. The Swatch phenomenon was launched in 1983 and continues to appeal to the public today.

The restructuring and the global success of Swatch allowed the Swiss watch-making industry to get back on its feet. Although quartz became a branch in its own right, the production of mechanical watches full of 'Swiss made' know-how restarted with a vengeance.

CHRONO

SWATCH – 1983

Launched in 1983, Swatch made a great contribution to saving the Swiss watchmaking industry from Japanese competition. Seven years after its official launch, a colourful range of chronographs appeared.

SEE OPPOSITE	1990 MODELS
MANUFACTURER	SWATCH
MODEL	CHRONO
REFERENCE	SIGNAL FLAG, FLASH ARROW, JELLY STAG
DIAL	COLOURED
WINDING MECHANISM	QUARTZ
CALIBRE	ETA
DIAMETER	36MM
MATERIAL	PLASTIC
STRAP	PLASTIC
TYPE	SIMPLE

SWATCH CHRONO CATALOGUE

The Swatch chronograph range launched in 1990 was particularly strong and colourful. Each model had a nickname.

- FLASH ARROW
- JELLY STAG
- WHITE HORSE
- NEO WAVE
- SKATE BIKE
- GRAND PRIX
- BLACK FRIDAY
- SIGNAL FLAG

COMING OUT OF THE QUARTZ CRISIS

From 1977 to 1983 the Swiss watch industry suffered a severe crisis as its exports were halved following the sudden appearance of Japanese quartz watches on the European market (see page 209). Against this background, Nicolas Hayek was asked to conduct a study on the industry's prospects. He concluded that it could not survive without relying on high-volume manufacturing and suggested a merger between two ailing companies: SSIH, which owned the makes Omega and Tissot, and ASUAG, the owner of Longines, Rado and ETA components. The merged company was first named Société de Microélectronique et d'Horlogerie (SMH). He then started a revolution with the launch of the first plastic quartz watch, made in Switzerland, in collaboration with Ernst Thomke, the head of ETA. Two of the company's engineers, Jacques Müller and Elmar Mock, had just developed a cheap, analogue (with hands) plastic quartz watch. In 1981, the new name was registered: Swatch – a portmanteau word formed from both 'Swiss' and 'watch' and 'second' and 'watch'. The idea was that this would convey its Swiss identity and appeal to owners of classic watches. Thanks to Hayek, the Swatch was commercially successful following its launch in the United States in 1982, and became the starting point for a global relaunch of the Swiss watch market. It was a fun watch with a classic design, it weighed just 20g and was waterproof to 30m. The mechanism was encased in plastic and appeared to be made out of a single piece. In fact, ultrasound was used to weld the Plexiglas glass to the case, which was initially made from ABS, a type of highly resistant plastic. The quartz movement, which in the first versions contained a total of 51 parts, was integrated with the back and could not be dismantled.

A GLOBAL SUCCESS

On 1 March 1983 the Swatch was launched in Europe. That year, 12 models were offered. Very quickly, almost 6,000 references, all different, were created and sold for the equivalent of £15 (50 Swiss francs). At the same time, SMH performed the feat of selling 1 million in the space of a year. When Swatch celebrated its 50th anniversary, the company announced that the 50,000,000th watch had been produced. In 1990, a Swatch collection with a chronograph complication was unveiled, as well as Scuba 200, a range of dive watches. The number and originality of the models offered, as well as the special series, cleverly orchestrated with dynamic advertising, contributed to producing a collector effect, which the brand's management were only too happy to encourage. In 1994, the Swatch Irony, made of steel, appeared and marked the start of a new era. The following year, the success of the steel versions gave rise to the launch of the aluminium models Chrono and Scuba. In 1997, the Skin, the world's thinnest plastic watch, was launched. In 1998, SMH became the Swatch Group. Fifteen years later, the launch of Sistem51, the first automatic watch, also made up of 51 parts, and whose manufacture was entirely automated, was a success. Since 2020 the brand has taken an environmentally responsible course, replacing plastic with bio-based materials.

MICKEY MOUSE & MOONSWATCH

SWATCH – 2018 & 2022

**Since its foundation in 1983, Swatch has always endeavoured to forge
inspiring artistic partnerships. In 2022, a union between
Speedmaster and Swatch made an impression.**

1. SEE OPPOSITE

MANUFACTURER	SWATCH × DAMIEN HIRST
MODEL	SPOT MICKEY FROM 2018
REFERENCE	N/A
DIAL	COLOURED
WINDING MECHANISM	QUARTZ
CALIBRE	ETA
DIAMETER	33MM
MATERIAL	PLASTIC
STRAP	PLASTIC
TYPE	SIMPLE

2. SEE OVERLEAF

MANUFACTURER	SWATCH × OMEGA
MODEL	MOONSWATCH FROM 2022
REFERENCE	MISSION TO NEPTUNE
DIAL	COLOURED
WINDING MECHANISM	QUARTZ
CALIBRE	ETA
DIAMETER	42MM
MATERIAL	BIOCERAMIC
STRAP	NYLON FABRIC
TYPE	VELCRO

SWATCH'S PARTNERSHIPS

Very quickly, the marketing genius Nicolas Hayek successfully fuelled the public's enthusiasm for Swatch watches with limited editions and variations on different, often artistic, themes. These moves contributed to making them cult objects for a whole generation. Indeed, the brand has always collaborated with numerous artists from different backgrounds. The list includes illustrators, painters and designers, such as Keith Haring, who first made an iconic pairing with Swatch in 1986. In 2018, the plastic watch celebrated 35 years of artistic partnerships. At the Swatch Art Peace Hotel in Shanghai, the company launched two models designed by the British artist Damien Hirst and made in honour of the 90th anniversary of Mickey Mouse. The Spot Mickey model, which was reminiscent of the watch made by Ingersoll in 1933 (see page 30), was a limited edition of 1,999, and sold out in a few hours. Today this Swatch watch is a collector's item.

MOONSWATCH

The MoonSwatch was the result of a joint project between the popular Swatch and the iconic Omega – both part of the Swatch Group. Released in 2022 and limited to certain outlets, it swept the board, flooding social media, discussion groups and watchmaking press coverage. This marvellous marketing coup – which led to stock shortages, long queues and high prices on specialist platforms – offered growing visibility to the two brands that had successfully joined forces while still retaining their respective identities. Nevertheless, despite the wild enthusiasm, it should be remembered that the 11 models offered in the catalogue were not officially limited editions. Priced at £200 (€250 – three times the price of a Swatch, but one-twentieth of the price of a standard Speedmaster), each MoonSwatch referenced an imaginary mission to a heavenly body in the solar system and was distinguished by a specific combination of colours. All faithfully shared the Speedmaster case (see page 98), but the material used, in keeping with Swatch's recent change of direction, was BioCeramic, which comprised a mix of two-thirds ceramic and one-third bio-derived plastic using the seeds of a castor plant. In a nod to the models that had been worn by astronauts, they featured a two-section Velcro nylon strap. As regards the mechanism they were not, of course, driven by the legendary calibre 321 (see page 101) but by a quartz movement, in keeping with the Swatch chronographs.

While some makes could not meet demand for their flagship models, Omega and Swatch took the opposite approach to the market. By making the iconic Speedmaster accessible to as many people as possible, this unprecedented partnership allowed customers to take their first step into the world of collectors' watches. Although the MoonSwatch was still a Swatch, not a mechanical Speedmaster, the operation was a resounding success.

FLIK FLAK LOUVRE

SWATCH – 1987

The first watch created specifically to teach children how to tell the time, Flik Flak remains the only children's watch made in Switzerland.

SEE OPPOSITE	**2021 MODEL**
MANUFACTURER	**SWATCH**
MODEL	**FLIK FLAK LOUVRE**
REFERENCE	**POWER TIME**
DIAL	**COLOURED**
WINDING MECHANISM	**QUARTZ**
CALIBRE	**ETA**
DIAMETER	**31MM**
MATERIAL	**BIO-BASED PLASTIC**
STRAP	**FABRIC**
TYPE	**SIMPLE**

CHILDPROOF WATCHES

Machine washable at 40° C (104° F): simply wrap in a sock and start the wash cycle.

No dangerous chemicals: each component has been tested to ensure it presents no risk to children.

Resistant to impact: the Swiss-made watch movement is safely ensconced in a robust plastic case and concealed behind a protective plastic dial.

Waterproof to 30m: children can therefore swim and bathe or shower while wearing their watches.

Made in Switzerland: each component, including the movement, is entirely manufactured in Switzerland.

CREATED WITH THE HELP OF TEACHERS

Flik Flak, which is owned by the Swatch Group, was created in 1987. It was designed in close collaboration with teachers and combined a look that appeals to very young people with a genuine educational concept. This unique tool for learning how to tell the time quickly became the most popular watch for children. The range has two categories.

The Story Time models, aimed at the youngest children, have two hands representing two characters: Flik (Mr Minutes) and Flak (Mrs Hour). Flik counts the minutes and likes to go forward every 60 seconds, while Flak loves to put her brother straight by reminding him that 60 minutes make an hour, and waits for her brother to take 60 steps forward before moving forward in turn.

The second family of watches, Power Time, is aimed at older children. These have three normal hands, with the minute hand uppermost, and dials that clearly display the 12 numerals with the intermediate intervals marked by dots. The colour of the hour hand matches that of the hour numerals, and that of the minute hand matches that of the minutes.

SWISS MADE

Flik Flak watches are high-end Swiss-made watches able to withstand whatever children can throw at them. Before going on sale, they spent a month in a specialized quality control laboratory where they underwent a battery of chemical and mechanical tests. When they went on the market, their quality standards exceeded legal requirements and bore the certification seal of the Consumer Product Safety Improvement Act (CPSIA). As part of the Swatch Group, the brand benefited from the experience and know-how of the world's biggest watch manufacturer.

UNPRECEDENTED PARTNERSHIPS

The Flik Flak range consists of a broad lineup of coloured watches aimed at children, where princesses, pirates, superheroes and explorers rub shoulders. There have also been numerous partnerships with other children's brands. In 2021, continuing its educational aims, Flik Flak launched a collection with the Louvre museum in Paris, putting the spotlight on the art of reading the time and hieroglyphics.

MACH 2000

LIP – 1975

In 1975, at the height of the LIP affair, and after being one of seven designers to get a call for help from the company, Roger Tallon created this piece to relaunch the Besançon-based manufacturer. It has become a cult item.

SEE OPPOSITE	2022 MODEL
MANUFACTURER	LIP
MODEL	MACH 2000
REFERENCE	670080
DIAL	BLACK
WINDING MECHANISM	QUARTZ
CALIBRE	RONDA 5021.D
DIAMETER	42 × 40MM
MATERIAL	STEEL
STRAP	LEATHER
TYPE	SIMPLE

CREATIONS BY LIP DESIGNERS

- RUDOLF MEYER | GALAXIE AND CARRÉE
- MARC HELD | LIP SKIPPER
- MICHEL BOYER | LIP CANDIDES
- ISABELLE HEBEY | RECTANGULAR WATCHES
- MICHEL KINN | GOLD-PLATED CARRÉE
- JEAN DINH VAN | SILVER
- ROGER TALLON | MACH 2000

A THREAT OF BANKRUPTCY

LIP is one of France's oldest watchmakers. Its history goes back to 1867, when Emmanuel Lipmann set up a watchmaking workshop in Besançon under his own name. It was an immediate success. His grandson, Fred, continued the tradition and, thanks to him, by 1932 it had become the number one brand in France. A symbol of French watchmaking, the LIP watch also helped to forge diplomatic ties: the French government presented a T18 watch as a gift to Winston Churchill after World War II. But at the end of the 1960s, LIP ran into financial difficulties. The year 1971 saw a turning point for the brand when Fred Lipmann was dismissed from the board. From 1973, as a result of competition from its Japanese competitors, who ceaselessly increased their market share (see page 209), the company faced bankruptcy and endured an unprecedented industrial dispute.

ROGER TALLON TO THE COMPANY'S RESCUE

In 1974, after a year's struggle, Michel Rocard, the first secretary of the French socialist party, sent Claude Neuschwander, formerly of advertising group Publicis, to negotiate with the unions. His mission was to relaunch the company, which was proud to have recently made the first French quartz watch movement. The watchmaker was taken over by its employees and, to mark the company's entry into a new era, Rocard engaged the services of the star designers of the day: Rudolf Meyer, Marc Held, Michel Boyer, Isabelle Hebey, Michel Kinn, Jean Dinh Van and France's most famous industrial designer, Roger Tallon.

The last of these had just left Technès, the agency where he had worked for 20 years, to set up his own studio. From now on, each of Tallon's projects was conceived using a systemic approach that examined the design in its entirety. Consequently, he was as interested in the ergonomics, colour, signage and packaging of an object, as well as its aesthetic appeal. In 1975, he used this approach to create the iconic Mach 2000, with its three coloured buttons.

FORM AND FUNCTION

For a modernist designer, form follows function. According to this principle, the half-moon shaped case of the Mach 2000 was created so that the wearer could bend their wrist comfortably. The hands, which contrasted with the dial, made it possible to tell the time at a distance of several metres. The rounded crowns prevented the owner from being injured by a sudden movement, and their colours made it possible to immediately identify the functions of the watch. Although its launch had been eagerly awaited, the Mach 2000 was not a success. Forty-five years later, the original version is sought after by collectors. As for the relaunched model, it has been a best seller for the brand, and has been exhibited in design meccas such as MoMA in New York and the Pompidou Centre in Paris.

OYSTERQUARTZ

ROLEX – 1977

**Long before the quartz crisis, Rolex had taken an interest in electronic technology.
In 1952, it registered a series of patents.**

SEE OPPOSITE	1986 MODEL
MANUFACTURER	ROLEX
MODEL	OYSTERQUARTZ
REFERENCE	19038
DIAL	GOLD
WINDING MECHANISM	QUARTZ
CALIBRE	5055
DIAMETER	36MM
MATERIAL	GOLD
STRAP	GOLD
TYPE	INTEGRATED

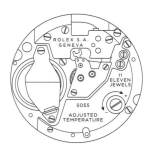

**ROLEX
CAL. 5055**

The Rolex calibres 5035 and 5055
appeared seven years after the Beta 21,
the first Swiss-made quartz movement. The
quality of their finish remains unmatched
among quartz watches.

PROJECT BETA 21

It was not the Astron, created in 1969 (see
page 226), that sowed panic in the Swiss
watchmaking industry. The threat had
materialized at the end of the 1950s, with the
appearance of Hamilton's electric watches
(see page 204), and the 1960 launch of the
Accutron, with its tuning fork movement
(see page 202). Faced with this competition,
manufacturers joined forces to organize a
fightback and create the first Swiss-made
quartz movement. In 1962, they jointly
founded the Centre Électronique Horloger
(CEH). This research team, set up by the
Fédération Horlogère, was co-funded by the
21 rival companies. In 1970, two years after
the first prototypes were made, the first
Rolex quartz watch went on sale. It was a
Date model, ref. 5100, but to accommodate
the new Beta 21 movement the case was
no longer the famous Oyster (see page
48). However, Rolex only sold 1,000 of
these watches as it wanted to market its
own movement. In 1977, after five years'
development, Rolex introduced its first
Oysterquartz movements, made entirely in-
house: the 5035 for the Datejust model and
the 5055 for the Day-Date.

QUARTZ MOVEMENTS MADE BY ROLEX

When they were released, the quartz models
5035 and 5055 were marvels of technology
and had a high-quality finish. They used
a specialized circuit – a 32 kHz oscillator
and analogue thermocompensation. That
meant that the watches were extremely
accurate, because the quartz was kept at
a constant temperature. Moreover, the
movements had a higher level of finish than
most mechanical movements: specifically,

they were adorned with *côtes de Genève*
(see page 29), a decoration usually found
on top-of-the-range mechanical movements.
When it came to their beauty and level of
finish, no other quartz movement could
compare. Rolex produced these watches
in different configurations: gold, steel and
Rolesor (gold and steel) until 2001. About
25,000 watches were sold until 2003.
In terms of design, these Rolex Oysterquartz
watches also featured a special case that
made it possible to accommodate the quartz
movement and an integrated strap.

A QUARTZ PERPETUAL CALENDAR THAT NEVER WENT ON SALE

Although the beginning of the 21st century
marked the end of the life of these models,
Rolex had nevertheless developed two specific
movements for the Oysterquartz: the 5335
and its variant, the 5355. Still destined for
the Datejust and Day-Date models, they
featured a perpetual calendar complication
(see page 171). For reasons known only to
Rolex, it was decided not to put them into
production, and the Oysterquartz line was
finally dropped when the last watches were
despatched from Geneva in 2003.

PULSAR

HAMILTON – 1970

**Unveiled on 6 May 1970, the Hamilton Pulsar was
the world's first digital watch with an LED display.**

SEE OPPOSITE	2022 MODEL
MANUFACTURER	HAMILTON
MODEL	PSR
REFERENCE	H52414130
DIAL	LCD/OLED
WINDING MECHANISM	DIGITAL QUARTZ
CALIBRE	N/A
DIAMETER	34.7 × 40.8MM
MATERIAL	STEEL
STRAP	STEEL
TYPE	INTEGRATED

FROM AN ORIGINAL IDEA BY STANLEY KUBRICK

The concept of a watch with a digital display first appeared in the movie *2001: A Space Odyssey*. In 1968, Stanley Kubrick asked the Hamilton Watch Company to create a watch for his film. Hamilton was the ideal choice (see page 204) as it was known for having made the first electric watch. After several prototypes, created under the direction of John Bergey, the collaboration yielded a watch with a futuristic design that featured a double analogue and digital display. Although the watch was not marketed until 2001 – a decision that was obviously in homage to the movie – Hamilton had been thinking about a revolutionary model along the lines of the concept dreamed up by the film director since 1970. The manufacturer joined forces with Electro/Data, a company that specialized in LED (light-emitting diode) technology, and set up Time Computer Inc., a subsidiary run by John Bergey. This venture produced the Pulsar: its name came from neutron stars, whose pulsations emit rays at an ultra-precise frequency. The watch was unveiled (and mocked) on the US television programme *The Tonight Show Starring Johnny Carson* in 1970, and went on sale in 1972.

'A WATCH THAT TAKES THE HARD TIME OUT OF TELLING TIME'

This was how the front page of the *New York Times* put it when the watch was launched. At the time, the Pulsar was the first watch to display the time digitally, using LEDs, and also the first electronic watch that had no moving parts. Instead, it contained 44 chips with an integrated circuit and 4,000 connecting wires; this ensured that it made use of the latest innovations at the time. The watch was an immediate success. Two versions were made in 1972: one in steel and one in gold, sold then at $2,100 (the equivalent of £13,000 today). About 10,000 were made, before enthusiasm evaporated with the arrival of LCD technology. Eventually, Hamilton sold its subsidiary to Time Computer Inc., which in turn was taken over by Seiko.

RETURN OF AN ICON

During the 1970s the popularity of the watch was such that it appeared on the wrists of the biggest celebrities. Inevitably, the industrialist Gianni Agnelli owned one. Other devotees were the boxer Joe Frazier and the musicians Elton John and Keith Richards. The best publicity came in 1973 when Roger Moore played James Bond for the first time in *Live and Let Die*. During the opening scene the spy wears a Pulsar, rather than his Submariner (see page 134) and, on two occasions, he explains how the push-button works. In 2020, 50 years after the first model, the German-Swiss manufacturer Hamilton relaunched a faithful reproduction of the watch, with a steel version and one in yellow gold with a PVD coating (see page 230). This time it featured a hybrid display combining a reflective LCD (liquid crystal display) screen and an OLED (organic light-emitting diode) screen that lit up.

G-SHOCK

CASIO – 1983

Far removed from the luxury world of Swiss watchmaking, the Japanese Casio brand stands out for of its tough but attractive products. A notable example is the G-Shock, which was unveiled in 1983.

SEE OPPOSITE	2021 MODEL
MANUFACTURER	CASIO
MODEL	G-SHOCK MADE IN JAPAN
REFERENCE	GW-5000
DIAL	LCD
REWINDING MECHANISM	DIGITAL QUARTZ
CALIBRE	MODULE 3159
DIAMETER	43MM
MATERIAL	STEEL + WITH DLC (DIAMOND-LIKE CARBON) TREATMENT
STRAP	POLYURETHANE
TYPE	SIMPLE

A FAMILY BUSINESS

In 1946, Tadao Kashio established Casio as Kashio Seisakujo. The company made a name for itself with an invention that was far removed from the world of watchmaking: the Yubiwa pipe – a cigarette-holder ring that made it possible to smoke a cigarette while working with both hands. Whatever one may think of it, it was a success, and the revenue it brought in allowed Casio to grow. The company then specialized in making components for microscopes and gearboxes, before becoming a leader in calculator design. In 1957, it was renamed Casio Computer. The company remained a family business, run by Shigeru Kashio and his three sons, Kazuo, Yukio and Tadao. Its calculators were initially used by research institutes before gaining wider appeal in 1972 with the Casio Mini. Following several crises, Casio Computer made use of its know-how to diversify its activities. It entered the watch market in 1974 with a model featuring a digital display (see page 16), the Casiotron. As well as displaying the time, it indicated the day and recognized leap years. Over the years different Casio watches came on the market, with mixed results, until the G-Shock came out in 1983.

THE TRIPLE 10 RULE

In 1981, Kikuo Ibe, a designer at Casio, set up a project management team of just three people to bring to fruition a concept dear to him: a watch that was so tough it would not break even if it were dropped. This idea came from an unfortunate experience: he had just smashed the watch given to him by his father.

There was no specific technical goal or schedule for the project, but there was one rule: Triple 10. The watch must withstand being dropped from a height of 10m, it must be waterproof to 10 bar (100m) and the battery must have a life of 10 years. Hundreds of prototypes were tested by being thrown out of his office window. One day, watching children playing with a rubber ball, Ibe had a eureka moment: to design a watch module that was almost loose, despite being held in place at certain points within a hollow structure. Like the children, the engineer tested this with a ball, and it worked. All that remained was to miniaturize the whole thing. In 1983, after two years of development and numerous destroyed prototypes, the G-Shock DW-5000 was unveiled and, with it, the concept of the shockproof watch became a reality.

130 MILLION SOLD

The watch Ibe had created, which was the fruit of painstaking development, was not an immediate success. One reason may have been that many shops were reluctant to sell an unbreakable watch. It was in the United States, thanks to some memorable commercials (including one in which the G-Shock was used as a hockey puck), that the watch's popularity began to grow. It quickly won over skateboarders, who were accustomed to falling, and surfers who wanted a waterproof watch. The fashion for streetwear contributed to the success of the watch during the 1990s. Since its launch in 1983, almost 130 million G-Shocks have been sold by Casio worldwide.

PROTECTION
CASIO
MULTI BAND 6
WR 20BAR
TOUGH SOLAR
ADJUST
MODE
LIGHT
RECEIVING
SNZ ALM SIG
L • M • H
ALARM
SHOCK RESIST
CHRONO
G-SHOCK

WORLD TIME

SEIKO – 1979

**A Japanese manufacturer founded in 1877,
Seiko is renowned for its perpetual search for accuracy.
It produced the first ever quartz watch.**

SEE OPPOSITE	2021 MODEL
MANUFACTURER	SEIKO
MODEL	G-SHOCK MADE IN JAPAN
REFERENCE	GW-5000
DIAL	LCD
WINDING MECHANISM	DIGITAL QUARTZ
CALIBRE	MODULE 3159
DIAMETER	43MM
MATERIAL	STEEL WITH DLC (DIAMOND-LIKE CARBON) TREATMENT
STRAP	POLYURETHANE
TYPE	SIMPLE

**SEIKO
QUARTZ MOVEMENT**

These watches are more accurate than
mechanical ones because the oscillator emits
a very precise signal: 32,768 Hz.

THE SEIKO FACTORY

The start of the Meiji era in 1868 allowed
Japan to open up to the West after two
centuries of isolation, and ushered the
country into the modern industrial world.
It was against this background, in 1877,
that 18-year-old Kintaro Hattori opened a
workshop in Tokyo. Business was good, and
in 1892 he bought a disused factory and
founded Seikosha (*Seiko* meaning 'success'
and *sha* 'house'). In 1895, Hattori produced
the Time Keeper, the first Japanese pocket
watch, and in 1913, despite competition,
he launched the Laurel, the first Japanese
wristwatch. Ten years later, the factory was
destroyed by an earthquake. It was rebuilt
a year later and the first model bearing the
Seiko brand name went on sale. Although
World War II caused further difficulties
for the company, it got back on its feet
afterwards. The 1950s were devoted to a
search for accuracy so that the company
could compete with the Swiss. In the 1960s,
Seiko reportedly announced that it had
sold more watches than all exports of Swiss
watchmaking in the same period.

THE ASTRON REVOLUTION

From the early 1950s, the company took
part in national watchmaking competitions.
Seiko quickly made its mark, and in
1958 its Marvel model was a sensation.
Seiko established its reputation in the
International Chronometry Competition
at the Neuchâtel observatory; it then
took the plunge with the tests run by the
prestigious Geneva observatory. From the
first time it participated, Seiko models won
second and third place in the Neuchâtel
and Geneva competitions. In five years,

the brand won fame going from 144th to
1st in their category. Although Seiko had
succeeded in establishing itself in the
mechanical watch sector, at the start of the
new decade the company's management
decided to concentrate on a new technology:
quartz. Although some laboratories had
been equipped with impressive quartz clocks
since 1940, the design for a wristwatch was
still a long way off. Seiko therefore still had
it all to do, and the company developed all
the components it needed itself, despite
difficulties with miniaturization and battery
life. By Christmas 1969, and after 10 years'
development, the first ever quartz watch –
the Astron – went on sale. Boasting accuracy
of losing only five seconds per month and
able to function continuously for a year, the
watch was 100 times more accurate and had
250 times more autonomy than any other
mechanical watch.

LCD DISPLAY

Although it revolutionized the market,
Seiko's management believed the Astron –
which looked like any other watch with three
hands – was too modest. From 1968, Seiko
took an interest in liquid crystal display
(LCD), and in 1973 the first quartz watch
with a six-figure LCD went on sale. In 1979,
Seiko launched the A239 World Time, one of
the first wristwatches to use two different
LCD modules: a screen displaying the
time and the day, and another displaying a
world map divided into time zones. Today,
the Seiko Watch Corporation produces two
separate makes: Seiko and Grand Seiko.
The latter, which has been independent since
2017, operates in the high horology sector;
its watches have set records for accuracy and
boast top-of-the-range levels of finish.

MAKES & MODELS

FACT SHEETS

WHO'S WHO

AUDEMARS, JULES-LOUIS: watchmaker who co-founded Audemars Piguet.

BELMONT, HENRY LOUIS: founder of Yema.

BERGEY, JOHN: head of development at Hamilton and in charge of Time Computer Inc. which made the Pulsar.

BIVER, JEAN-CLAUDE: head of a high horology company that took part in the rescue of Blancpain and other manufacturers.

BOVET, JEAN-FRÉDÉRIC: father of Frédéric, Alphonse and Édouard, and founder of the Bovet company.

BOVET, FRÉDÉRIC, ALPHONSE and ÉDOUARD: sons of Jean-Frédéric, who contributed to the success of the Bovet brand.

BRANDT, LOUIS: founder of the watchmaking factory that became Omega.

BREGUET, ABRAHAM-LOUIS: a watchmaking genius who contributed to revolutionizing all aspects of the industry. The Breguet company continues this tradition.

BREITLING, LÉON: founder of the Breitling company.

BREITLING, GASTON and WILLY: respectively the second and third generations at the helm of Breitling.

BULOVA, JOSEPH: American watchmaker who founded the Bulova company.

CARTIER, LOUIS-FRANÇOIS: renowned French jeweller, founder of Cartier.

CARTIER, ALFRED LOUIS and LOUIS JOSEPH: respectively second and third generations at the helm of the Cartier company.

CHAUVOT, RENÉ-ALFRED: inventor of the Reverso case.

CONSTANTIN, FRANÇOIS: businessman who started Vacheron Constantin with Jacques-Barthélémy Vacheron.

CORVO, GIORGIO: Italian businessman who contributed to the revival of the Jaeger-LeCoultre Reverso.

COUSTEAU, JACQUES-YVES: French naval officer and oceanographic explorer.

CZAPEK, FRANÇOIS: watchmaker who founded Czapek & Cie, forerunner of Patek Philippe.

DELAUZE, HENRI: founder of the Comex company.

DESCOMBES, NUMA-ÉMILE: co-founder of Universal Genève.

DE MARCHI, CARLO: famous distributor of watches in Italy.

DE PATEK, ANTOINE NORBERT: Polish watchmaker, naturalized Swiss, who started the Patek Philippe company with Czapek.

DE TREY, CÉSAR: distributor of Swiss watches who was behind the idea of a watch that could be turned over: the Reverso.

DITISHEIM FAMILY: founded the Vulcain watchmaking company.

DUCOMMUN, GEORGES: founder of the Doxa company.

ESCHLE, URS: in charge of developing the Doxa Sub.

FAVRE-JACOT, GEORGES: founder of Zenith (originally Georges Favre-Jacot et Cie).

FIECHTER, JEAN-JACQUES: managing director of Blancpain from 1950 to 1980, responsible for the Fifty Fathoms.

GENTA, GÉRALD: renowned watch designer.

GLEITZE, MERCEDES: British swimmer, holder of several records, whose swim across the English Channel helped to popularize the Rolex Oyster.

GOLAY, GEORGES: manager of Audemars Piguet, responsible for the Royal Oak.

HARWOOD, JOHN: inventor of the first automatic wristwatch.

HATTORI, KINTARO: Japanese watchmaker, founder of the Seiko company.

HAWLEY, ROBERT and CHARLES, HENRY: founders of the Ingersoll company.

HAYEK, NICOLAS: Swiss entrepreneur, president of the Swatch Group, who worked to save the Swiss watchmaking industry.

HEUER, ÉDOUARD: watchmaker who founded the Heuer company.

HEUER, CHARLES-AUGUSTE AND JACK: respectively second and third generations at the helm of Heuer.

HETZEL, MARC: Swiss engineer, recruited by Bulova, head of the Accutron programme.

HYSEK, JÖRG: watch designer who created the Vacheron 222.

IBE, KIKUO: inventor of the Casio G-Shock.

JAEGER, EDMOND: French watchmaker, designer with Cartier, who worked with LeCoultre & Cie, which became Jaeger-LeCoultre.

JEANNERET, RENÉ-PAUL: historical figure in the Rolex company, responsible for the marketing of many watches.

JONES, FLORENTINE ARIOSTO: founder of the International Watch Company and inventor of the Jones calibre.

LECOULTRE, JACQUES DAVID: fourth generation at the helm of the LeCoultre & Cie company. Founded Jaeger-LeCoultre with Edmond Jaeger.

LESCHOT, GEORGES-HENRY: genius watchmaker and mechanic who joined Vacheron Constantin and contributed to its rise.

LIPMANN, EMMANUEL: founder of the LIP company.

LIPMANN, ERNEST and FRED: respectively second and third generations at the helm of the LIP company.

LUCKEY, GEORGE: head of research and development at Hamilton, who contributed to the creation of the Ventura.

MALOUBIER, ROBERT: member of the French armed forces who was in charge of setting up a unit of combat swimmers and equipping them with watches. He contributed to the development the Fifty Fathoms.

PERRET, ULYSSE GEORGES: co-founder of Universal Genève.

PICCARD, AUGUSTE: Swiss physicist, pilot and sailor.

PIGUET, EDWARD-AUGUSTE: watchmaker and co-founder of Audemars Piguet.

PIQUEREZ, ERVIN: inventor of waterproofing devices named Compressor and Super-Compressor.

RACINE, ARISTE and ARISTE JR: founding family of the watch manufacturer Enicar.

ROBERT, FRÉDÉRIC: founder of the Aquastar company and consultant to Omega.

SANTOS-DUMONT, ALBERTO: Brazilian aviation pioneer.

SCHILD-COMTESSE, RUDOLF: manager of the family business Eterna (Schild Frères).

SEISAKUJO FAMILY: founding family of the Casio company.

STERN FAMILY: Patek Philippe has been in the hands of the Stern family, which has run it from father to son, since 1932 (Jean and Charles; Henri; Philippe; Thierry).

TALLON, ROGER: French designer who created the LIP Mach 2000.

THOMKE, ERNST: businessman who contributed to the restructuring of the Swiss watch industry at the height of the quartz crisis.

TORNEK, ALAIN: American distributor of Blancpain watches.

VACHERON, JACQUES-BARTHÉLÉMY: founder of the manufacturer Vacheron Constantin with François Constantin.

VERMOT, CHARLES: watchmaker who worked on the Zenith El Primero movement.

WILSDORF, HANS: manager and creator of the Rolex brand.

WITTNAUER, ALBERT: founder of the Wittnauer company, which sold watches.

WHAT'S WHAT

AMPLITUDE: the angle traced by a watch's balance, from its resting position to its extreme positions. Generally speaking the amplitude of a balance is between 180 degrees and 315 degrees.

ANTIMAGNETIC: this term refers to a watch where the function of the regulating components is not affected by magnetism.

APERTURE (OR WINDOW): an opening in the dial that allows information to be displayed.

ATM: abbreviation of 'atmosphere'. A unit of pressure that indicates how waterproof a watch is (10 atm = 100m).

ATOMIC CLOCK: a clock with extremely high accuracy. Its oscillating device uses the frequency of radiation emitted between two levels of energy of atoms.

BALANCE SPRING: together, the balance spring and balance are the very heart of a watch. Between them they regulate the functioning of time with their oscillation, and are responsible for the accuracy of a watch.

BALANCE: a circular mobile component that oscillates on its rotational axis. The balance is partnered with the balance spring and imparts a back-and-forth (tick-tock) movement, dividing time into equal segments.

BARREL: cylindrical component with toothed edges that contains the mainspring or spiral.

BEZEL: a ring fitted over the central part of the case. It is used to record extra information, such as the duration of an event.

BRIDGE: a plate attached to the main plate, on which one of the pivots of the moving parts of the movement turns.

CALIBRE: term that designates the type of movement used in a watch.

CASE: the chief protection of a watch, it keeps the movement safe from impacts, damp and dust.

CHEMIN DE FER: see 'railway track'.

CHRONOGRAPH: a precision watch featuring a counter that allows it to measure and display time intervals.

CLOUS DE PARIS: a motif that may feature on engraved dials.

COMPLICATION: any function a watch may have apart from showing hours, minutes and seconds.

COSC: Contrôle Officiel Suisse des Chronomètres – the official Swiss chronometer testing institute.

CROWN: a winding device outside the case that makes it possible to rewind the movement manually or to set the time.

DATE: the display of the date, either via a rotating disc or a hand, indicating the number of the day in the current month.

DAUPHINE: a hand in the shape of an elongated lozenge.

DIAL: the surface on which the hours, minutes, seconds and other useful pieces of information are marked.

ÉBAUCHE: a collection of components of a movement that has not been assembled, sold as such.

ENGRAVING: a technique for decorating dials.

ESCAPEMENT: a mechanical component located between the energy source and the regulating mechanism.

FLUTING: grooves found on crowns, making it possible to grip them more firmly, and on bezels and certain cases for visual effect.

FLYBACK: function that makes it possible to start timing a new event when the chronograph is already running to time another.

FOLDING: a type of buckle found on watch straps. It is hinged and unfolds when it is undone.

FREQUENCY: the number of vibrations made by the balance in an hour (measured in hertz).

GEAR TRAIN: part of the movement of a watch.

GMT: Greenwich Mean Time. The solar time at the meridian that passes through the Greenwich Observatory in the UK.

HAMMER: a metal component that strikes gongs to make them vibrate and thus produce sounds.

INDEX: a mark indicating hours on the dial of a watch.

JUMPING HOUR: an hour displayed through an aperture, invented by Blondeau in the 1830s.

LÉPINE: a pocket watch named after its inventor, whose crown is at 12 o'clock.

LUG: situated at either end of the case, lugs are where the strap is attached.

LUMINOVA: the latest generation of luminous paste, applied to hands and numerals, which absorbs light and releases it in darkness.

MAIN PLATE: a component that supports the bridges and the parts of a mechanical movement, on which the dial rests.

MECHANICAL WATCH: a watch with a mechanical movement, which does not need a battery to function.

MICRO-ROTOR: a small rotor contained within the calibre.

MIDDLE: one of the three main components of the case and the part that houses the movement. Located between the caseback and the bezel.

MINUTE REPEATER: a mechanism that chimes the time on demand when a push-button or a screw is pressed.

MOON PHASE: a watch complication that allows the various phases of the moon to be displayed on the dial.

MOTION WORK: a gear train behind the dial that transmits the rotation of the minutes pinion to the hour hand.

MOVEMENT: all the components that enable a watch to function.

NATO: a type of fabric watch strap.

OSCILLATION: the back-and-forth movement of a balance between two extreme positions.

PALLETS: internal component of a mechanical movement, attached to the escapement.

POWER RESERVE: the duration of a movement's function when its barrel spring is wound to the maximum.

PULSOMETER: a chronograph featuring a scale that gives the number of heartbeats per minute.

PUSH-BUTTON: a button that is pushed to start a mechanism.

PVD: Physical Vapor Deposition. A process for treating surfaces, borrowed from industry, to make metallic coatings for watchmaking products.

QUARTZ: a watch that uses an electronic oscillator, controlled by a quartz crystal resonator.

RADIUM: a radioactive material used on watch hands and indexes until the 1960s.

RAILWAY TRACK: a minutes scale printed on the dial that resembles railway tracks.

ROTOR: a semi-circular disc pivoting freely under the action of each of the arm's movements, whose function is to coil the driving spring automatically. Also known as an oscillating weight.

RUBY: a stone used in watchmaking that makes it possible to minimize the effects of friction. Originally, real rubies were used; these have been replaced by synthetic stones.

SAPPHIRE: a type of glass used in watches which, unlike Plexiglas, is resistant to scratching.

SAVONNETTE (HUNTER): a pocket watch with a cover to protect the glass, dial and hands; the crown is located at 3 o'clock.

SECOND HAND: it advances in jumps and follows the oscillation of the balance.

SECOND: subsidiary seconds are a function that makes it possible to indicate seconds in a different way on a dial (at 6 o'clock or 9 o'clock), unlike sweep seconds, where the axis is located at the centre.

SONNERIE (CHIME): an acoustic device that indicates hours and minutes, and even quarter hours and minutes, automatically or on demand.

SPRING: the source of mechanical energy in a watch, generally a hardened and blued steel ribbon coiled inside the barrel.

TACHYMETER: a chronograph with a scale that makes it possible to read speed in kilometres per hour or other units.

TELEMETER: a chronograph with a scale that makes it possible to measure the distance between an event and the point from which it is observed using the speed of sound.

TONGUE: the commonest type of strap fastening.

TOURBILLON: a complex mechanism, perfected by Breguet in 1801, in order to compensate for discrepancies in functioning caused by the earth's gravitational field. Its components are contained in a mobile cage.

TRITIUM: a luminous material used on hands and indexes until replaced by Luminova.

TUNING FORK: a small component with two parallel arms, welded together in a 'U' shape and attached to a shaft. It enables a movement fitted with it to attain unequalled accuracy of (it loses) a minute a month.

UNIVERSAL TIME: a complication, invented by Louis Cottier, which allows a watch to display the time in the world's 24 time zones simultaneously.

VIBRATION: a balance's movement between two extreme positions. A balance makes five oscillations per second, 18,000 per hour, for a frequency de 2.5 Hz.

WATCHMAKING WORKS: a company that has the expertise to manufacture its watches without using subcontractors. Since many companies use *ébauches*, the term has become looser in its application.

ABOUT THE AUTHOR

Clément Mazarian was born at the end of the 1980s. From the moment his grandfather gave him his first watch, a Seamaster, he developed a strong passion for horology. He learned from the most experienced collectors and dealers, and completed his knowledge via the internet and specialist forums. Clément bought watches, but sold them on. His discoveries were noticed by expert collectors and, in 2015, he founded his company and offered old watches for sale on his Instagram account (@collection.personnelle).

Over time he has diversified, but watches are still at the centre of what he does. Since 2020 he has been a consultant for the fashion magazine *L'étiquette*, for which he writes articles. With this book, Clément hopes to share his love for horology and 20th-century design, while also telling the stories behind the cult watches of our time.

WATCHMAKING LITERATURE

- *Art of Breguet*, G. Daniels, Philip Wilson Publishers, 2021
- *Chronomaster Only*, G. Rossier, A. Marquié, Watchprint.com, 2018
- *Collecting Nautilus and Patek Philippe*, O. Patrizzi, G. Mondani, Mondani, 2015
- *Flightmaster Only*, G. Rossier & A. Marquié, Watchprint.com, 2018
- *Heuer Autavia Chronographs 1962-85*, R. Crosthwaite, P. Gavin, Blurb, 2021
- *Heuer Carrera Chronographs 1963-85*, R. Crosthwaite, P. Gavin, Blurb, 2021
- *Heuer Monaco – Design Classic*, R. Crosthwaite, P. Gavin, Blurb, 2021
- *Moonwatch Only*, G. Rossier, A. Marquié, Watchprint.com, 2019
- *Navitimer Story*, G. Rossier, A. Marquié, Watchprint.com, 2022
- *Omega: voyage à travers le temps* (*Omega: a Journey through Time*), M. Richon, Marco Richon, 2007
- *Omega Seamaster Vintage*, A. Isnardi, Isnardi Editore, 2019
- *Patek Philippe Steel Watches*, J. Goldberger, Damiani, 2013
- *Swatch: Le Guide du connaisseur et du collectionneur*, (*Swatch: A Guide for Connoisseurs and Collectors*) F. Edwards, Soline, 1998
- *The Art of Patek Philippe*, Antiquorum, 1998
- *The Secrets of Vacheron Constantin*, F. Cologni, D. Fléchon, Flammarion, 2006
- *The Vintage Rolex Datejust Buyer's & Collector's Guide*, T. van Straaten, 2022
- *The Watch Book: Rolex*, G. L. Brunner, teNeues, 2021
- *Time For a Change: Discovering Vintage Enicar*, M. van der Ven, 2020
- *Universal Genève – Ten*, R. Crosthwaite, P. Gavin, Blurb, 2021

WEBSITES AND BLOGS

antiquorum.swiss
bobswatches.com
chronographes.net
chronomaddox.com
collectability.com
forumamontres.forumactif.com
fratellowatches.com
gmtmaster1675.com
hautehorlogerie.org
hodinkee.com
lecalibre.com
leclubyema.fr
lepetitpoussoir.fr
lesrhabilleurs.com
moonphase.fr
omegaforums.net
omegapassion.com
onthedash.com
passion-horlogere.com
phillips.com
rolexmagazine.com
universalgenevepolerouter.com
watch-wiki.net
watchbooksonly.com
worldtempus.com

ACKNOWLEDGEMENTS

My warmest thanks to Romain Réa and his team who have contributed to this book,
especially Daniel Coffaro, Jérôme Lemoine and Julien Bon. I would like to thank the professionals and
private collectors who allowed me to complete this selection of watches: Clotilde Rafine-Ricard, Nicolas Amsellem,
Gabriel Vachette, Gregoire Sierro, Gregoire Rossier, Anthony Marquié, Marc Beaugé, Gauthier Borsarello,
Jules Mesny-Deschamps, Edouard Schumacher, Alejandro Monroy and others who wish to remain nameless.
Finally, thank you to the watchmakers Jean-Louis Strack, Bryan Durand and Roberto Tarabella.

Many thanks to Anoush and Henry for their help. Thank you to all the team at Les éditions du Chêne
(Emmanuel, Faris, Sabine and Benoit) for their confidence in me. Thank you to Julie for her remarkable work.
And huge thanks to my family, especially my parents and my wife, Marilyn.

Finally, I dedicate this book to Jules and Léona, hoping that my passion
for watches is conveyed to them.

Originally published as *Collection Personnelle* by Editions du Chêne – Hachette Livre

First published in Great Britain in 2024 by Mitchell Beazley, an imprint of
Octopus Publishing Group Ltd, Carmelite House, 50 Victoria Embankment, London EC4Y 0DZ
www.octopusbooks.co.uk

An Hachette UK Company
www.hachette.co.uk

Distributed in the US by Hachette Book Group, 1290 Avenue of the Americas, 4th and 5th Floors, New York, NY 10104
Distributed in Canada by Canadian Manda Group, 664 Annette St.,Toronto, Ontario, Canada M6S 2C8

ISBN 978 1 78472 944 8
A CIP catalogue record for this book is available from the British Library.

Printed in China
1 3 5 7 9 10 8 6 4 2

For Editions du Chêne:
Photographer: Henry Leutwyler
Managing Editor: Emmanuel Le Vallois
Publisher: Faris Issad
Editor: Julie Mege
Art Director: Sabine Houplain
Retouching: TJ Huff for Henry Leutwyler Studio, NYC
Illustrations: Derudderdesign
Production: Rémy Chauvière
Photogravure: Quadrilaser
Press relations: presse_chene@hachette-livre.fr

For Mitchell Beazley:
Publisher: Alison Starling
Senior Managing Editor: Sybella Stephens
Translation from French: Simon Jones
Copy Editor: Julie Brooke
Creative Director: Jonathan Christie
Designer: Jeremy Tilston